for Mary, Magi and family —
I hope this little
book is a blessing — it
was a joy for me to write.
God bless you richly!
♥ Pastor Sharon

3

GOOD
(ENOUGH)
PEOPLE

SHARON M. LATOUR PH.D.

Also by Dr. Latour:

Radical Wholeness: A Pastor's Perspective

ISBN: 1475030711

ISBN-13: 9781475030716

CreateSpace, North Charleston, SC

TABLE OF CONTENTS

Much love and many thanks to Dad and Mom, who said it wouldn't be easy and did their best to prepare us for The Ride.

It was absolutely good enough.

INTRODUCTION

Good (enough) People suggests there are people who are good. In fact, chapter by chapter, we're reminded that we are all good (enough) people. Believing we are good or not, is the fundamental premise that drives everything else in life. It determines whether we will be kind or cruel, generous or stingy, patient or smoldering, all day long.

It is a fundamental issue of identity, with personal and global implications.

But it's not enough to merely tell you it's better to believe you are good (enough) than not. In working with clay, there's a lovely overarching metaphor which is a compelling parallel to our humanity that may convince you *why* you can genuinely reimagine giving yourself and your neighbor, a break.

I wrote this book to be gentle in asking the reader, younger or older, to reconsider what we already believe about our Selves. There are some unfortunate theories taught, even in esteemed academic and theological places, which are tragically keeping us from the fullness of our miraculous lives.

But there are also emerging pockets of newer thinking, that validate Wisdom from ancient sources, now becoming available for our incorporation.

A new way of thinking about how to hold our lives, especially when we are older, is one of the most important things we'll ponder. The impact the lives of community elders can have on younger people is incalculable, for both elders and youth, enlivening the entire community.

Through the use of clay dynamics as metaphor for our humanity, I hope you'll have enough "space" to willingly reimagine your unique and worthwhile life. As with all metaphors, "a thing that represents something else, though not literally," a clay analogy has its limits. But, taken as far as is reasonable, it is delightfully and surprisingly useful.

As an introduction to our clay-for-humanity metaphor, Kristin Muller's *The Potter's Studio Handbook* is illustrative:

"Potters often refer to clay as having memory. The concept is fairly simple: Clay likes to return to its original shape...For example, when a slab of clay is rolled out in only one direction, as it dries it will tend to pull back to the direction from which it was rolled...It is important not to disfigure vessels when handling, because although they can be reshaped, as the piece dries it will disfigure slightly again in the firing."[1]

Clay wonderfully mimics how both malleable and delicate we can be: and that we each have a unique nature about us. There is already a "distinctly you" about you. And the high heat of life reveals who we are, have been, and are still discovering within our Selves.

Both formal education and experience tell me that it's only when we fully embrace our lives that we might see past our sense of isolation to extend a mature and thoughtful embrace to the community just outside our door. In the following pages, we'll hear from several Wisdom teachers and reconsider our limiting beliefs about ourselves and others, and be truly free to celebrate who we are as absolutely good enough.

And that is all we ever need to be.

CHAPTER ONE
PERFECT
IMPERFECTION

"In most cultures, stories of the creation of human beings speak of our origins in clay."
~ Brother Iain Highet

Porcelain mugs by Elaine Shore

These mugs have been wood or electric kiln-fired. Generally judged as "imperfections" in an electric kiln, the random ash drips on the wood-fired mug (foreground) creates uniquely remarkable and highly-prized beauty.

A compelling reason to use clay as metaphor to begin rethinking cultural assumptions about our lives is *because it's not really you, but it can act a lot like you.* While clay has wonderful complexities and individual "behavior," it's absolutely, positively, not your actual Self.

You don't have to take my observations about clay personally.

Throughout this journey, I'll deliberately ease into addressing our renewal possibilities by defining something about how dirt can become a magically resilient, astonishingly beautiful, and even functional work of art. It's like an ongoing parable or "once-upon-a-time" story.

In the well-expressed foreword to Kristen Muller's *The Potter's Studio Handbook*, Brother Iain Highet helps make the tie between us and clay:

"To work with clay is to accept forever being a beginner...In every moment of the clay process---wedging, centering, throwing, forming, painting, glazing, and firing---there is an engagement with primal and elemental forces that awaken something at the origin and center of our humanity. Earth, water, fire, and the breath of life we potters give with our hands---these are the elements of working with clay...It is found in nearly every civilization, all over the world, in one form or another. And in most cultures, stories of the creation of human beings speak of our origins in clay." [2]

Many of us are overwhelmed: utterly spent and tired. We have compassion fatigue when it comes to caring for others, and have none at all left for ourselves. The popular press tells us all this; that we are feeling more and more isolated, despite immediate technological access to anyone at any time or place.

We've become human doings; forgetting our human beingness. And we don't want to think about it, much less talk about it.

Respecting our reluctance to tackle the place we collectively find ourselves in the second decade of the new millennium, using metaphors for our humanity, in our case, ceramics, might make our journey more inviting.

Described as "a problem-solving approach" by life coach Martha Beck, metaphors are great gifts. Because language can be limiting and labels confining, metaphors open up possibilities; relaxing us to be able to imagine and synthesize to surprising degrees.

Moreover, because of language limits, using clay as a metaphor, an everyday element that can be *physically* experienced, is particularly helpful:

"Humans, with our highly developed language skills, have a unique ability to think in metaphors... The key to understanding all the astonishing puzzle solutions created by the human Imagination, every human insight or innovation for navigating the wild world, boils down to the little concept *this is like that*. In every ancient wisdom tradition, wayfinders are taught to see metaphors in everything and to use metaphor to solve the puzzles that face humanity...Asian mystics said enlightenment was *like* the moon reflected in a thousand teacups, *like* an uncarved wooden block, *like* a cloudless sky. Jesus, the world's all-time most popular wayfinder, was a veritable geyser of metaphors: "The kingdom of heaven is *like* a treasure...*like* a mustard seed, *like* a pearl, *like* yeast..." I'm sure if Jesus were a modern American, He could tell us how the kingdom of heaven is like a Laundromat, an Olympic bobsled team, a double order of fries and a Coke. The guy was a metaphor machine."[3]

Metaphor, especially humorous metaphor, loosens up our air-tight beliefs and makes new thinking possible. Our human life *can be like* the ceramic process.

Parker Palmer, a widely published teacher-mentor, confessed to deep clinical depression in mid-life; a result of not wanting to think about or talk about his "divided" (or inauthentic) life.

We'll hear more from this Quaker friend later, but here's how he described his experience of discovery about true Self.

"For a long time, the "oughts" had been the driving force in my life---and when I failed to live "up" to those oughts, I saw myself as a weak and faithless person. I never stopped to ask, "How does such-and-such fit my God-given nature?" or "Is such-and-such truly my gift and call?" As a result, important parts of the life I was living were not mine to live and thus were doomed to fail...

After hours of careful listening, my therapist offered an image that helped me eventually reclaim my life. "You seem to look upon depression as the hand of an enemy trying to crush you," he said. "Do you think you could see it instead as the hand of a friend, pressing you down to ground on which it is safe to stand?"[4]

With that profoundly honest, imagery-filled teaching in mind, and aware that the messiness of our lives is often inconvenient in forcing us to adjust our striding pace, our first encounter with clay-as-grounding-material offers gently profound encouragement and insight.

Tony Birks, in *The Complete Potter's Companion*, uses ceramic artist language to describe clay properties. But notice how he could just as easily be describing our everyday reality as he vividly reveals clay's basic beginnings:

"Clay is weathered granite...where clay lies deep in beds near its origin, it is likely to be fairly pure...all its descendants contain impurities and, funnily enough, it is the impurities which give clays their character and value for the potter, affecting color and texture...the potter does not have to be a chemist to discover that the more "impure" the clay, the better working quality it may have... The clay needs "conditioning" by years of exposure to the weather..."[5]

Many potters notice that the purest porcelain is not nearly as interesting, when glazes of various colors are applied, as "impure" clay, like the earthenware bodies, that contain iron and other minerals. That it is actually "the impurities which give clays their character and value."

Before committing a beautiful piece of work to a particular glaze, Master Potters fire "test tiles" to calibrate clay bodies and glazes in combination. This helps take the guesswork out of what will later emerge from the kiln.

And despite all the science and experience, potters know there will be completely unexpected surprises, due to things still out of their control like: how that clay body will react to the heat reduction process; or where that piece sat in the kiln; and what specific glazed pieces it sat next to during high firing.

Even clay is impacted by the company it keeps.

But Porcelain, while the purest and most predictable with which to work, for many potters, often becomes less interesting an artistic adventure. Pretty Porcelain has her loveliness and breathtaking beauty to offer the world. But I already know her, and I'm more interested in the surprises that await every time I work with an impure clay body. (That's how potters speak about a clay's composition: a clay body.)

It is the very "imperfection" in the clay that makes it stunningly unique and stimulating as heat and various glazes work on it. It is the lead and sand and other minerals that give it resilience and character.

So, what if we could imagine that the Self we are, "talents" and "flaws" together, is plenty good enough? That we might quiet the persistent panel of judges in our heads, and entertain the possibility that we are perfect as we are in the Self we inhabit; to be exactly who we are equipped to be as a vital member of our community.

Previously cited writer and life coach, Martha Beck, is also a wife and mother. Like Henri Nouwen, the priest who wrote extensively out of his own brokenness and gave himself the title "Wounded Healer," Dr. Beck's most recent publication entitled *Finding Your Way in a Wild New World,* suggests our pain is grist for the healing mill for the sake of the world.

Like Buddhist nun Pema Chodron who helps North Americans appreciate ways of developing compassion, after wondering out loud what to call them, Beck calls the eyes-wide-open elders, "menders and wayfinders."

One thing I've picked up in this most recent book is how Beck marvels at her teenage son Adam. (Interestingly, "Adamah," the first man, means "out of clay.") She wrote an earlier book about deciding to deliver Adam against all Harvard University peer pressure, when she discovered he had the extra chromosome that causes Down syndrome. You can hear sadness, wonder, duty, loneliness and determination in those *Expecting Adam* pages.

But, by her own assessment, that very book launched her career. Adam, by simply being "imperfect" has made a world of difference for a woman who, otherwise, might have become just another over-educated academic instead of a profound game changer.

In *Finding Your Way in a Wild New World*, now-grown Adam accompanies his mom's group on a life coaching safari to Africa. It is clear she realizes Adam's difference is mystical, and is making all the difference in Beck's over-educated, over-thinker's life. It's a joy to hear the wonder in her recent writing as she experiences a Self in Adam that is beyond her ability to understand or explain or control.

We know Beck's growth journey between *Expecting Adam* and *Finding Your Way in a Wild New World* could not have been easy. But we can be sure the fifteen years since Adam was born have made a significant difference in Beck's outlook on life.

She was one who struggled with eating disorders and tried to be the best little girl in the world: a perfect porcelain doll. Adam's uniquenesses seem to have helped burst her careful little world wide open into one of unlimited considerations and opportunities.

Perfect imperfection.

I draw on Martha Beck's story, an account of a public person who has written extensively out of her own life, so we might appreciate the helpfulness of her journey for ourselves. Our perspective is expanded through such poignant tales.

That is the gift of parable and story, to help us gently imagine possibilities where we had closed doors and options for ourselves or others: to better appreciate our perfectly imperfect and unique clay bodies.

So we'll keep drawing from stories and parables and metaphors.

CHAPTER TWO
SENSE OF HOME

"A studio is a workspace...it will (and should) get dirty."[6]

The Arcata Fire Arts Center is a controlled-chaos, second home to many.

For some ceramic artists, "place" is a priority; for others, only a practical necessity. But, all agree that clay work is messy, dusty, and muddy.

So potters are intentional in beginning the creation process.

A sense of home is key to some and more incidental to others. But no matter what, all agree that the Act of Creation is messy. Very, very messy.

And just like ceramic artistry, whether we admit it or like it or not, life is every bit as messy. Since no one is an island,[1] we accept that we live within a larger social context. And in practical terms, we need each other for survival. At one level or another, we live in relationship to an often untidy and sometimes contentious community.

In a new and challenging book, *Falling Upward: A Spirituality for the Two Halves of Life*, Richard Rohr supports the key possibility we'll examine throughout this book:

Those who decide to embrace the authentic Self and the whole of their lives can become the elders, the menders, the wayfinders, the wounded healers, and mentors for the sake of their peer and especially the young people.

In order to redeem our lives (meaning the radical deepest work of resolving what we might term yesterday's missteps, sins, mistakes, etc.) so

---

1 "No man is an island, entire of itself; every man is a piece of the continent, a part of the main. If a clod be washed away by the sea, Europe is the less, as well as if a promontory were, as well as if a manor of thy friends or of thine own were: any man's death diminishes me, because I am involved in mankind, and therefore never send to know for whom the bells tolls; it tolls for thee." John Donne, 1624

that we can live into the richest and most hope-filled days of our lives ahead, we must first establish a sense of what we mean by our genuinely safe place called "home."

We all need a safe and welcoming place to land.

And how we define "home" requires the greatest care. Home can refer to so many important "places." It can go from being an actual geographical location on a physical map, to an idea or concept of space to dance within a relationship. It includes how we feel in our own body.

In his chapter entitled, "Home and Homesickness," Rohr, forty years a Franciscan Brother, uses Homer's story of Odysseus's long and treacherous journey that eventually led him back home, after Odysseus was able to stop all his messy, frenetic activity and searching, and turn inward to the subtlety of wise discernment within.

"But the first half of his life was necessary to lead into his second half, "Now he can *go home* because he has, in fact, *come home* to his true and full self. His sailing and oaring days of mere "outer performance" are over, and he can now rest in the simplicity and ground of his own deeper life. He is free to stop his human *doing* and can at last enjoy his human *being*."[7] (Italics in original.)

This is lovely encouragement for second-half-of-lifers. If we choose to regard our lives with a softer, gentler gaze, as people who believe we were ultimately created in love to be Beloved, the redemption possibilities are unlimited, and personal awareness of purposes served by past events become continuous blessings.[2]

But there's an equally compelling rationale for community elders to reconsider their lives in the light of compassion: The young people.

Many, many elders slowly shake their heads when asked what they'd say to the younger version of themselves. In one way or another, they suggest they'd tell themselves to lighten up, that things work out, that they will be ok.

We longed for guides, for gentle Wisdom teachers, to companion us on the path of this profoundly mystifying life adventure.

The places where we are formed can appear to be tidy or messy...because no two potter's studios are alike. And as our lives are being formed, with all the questions about Self and others still evolving, dust is often chaotically flying. And those early storms can be blinding and frightening.

Rohr's multidisciplinary approach to discussing home is broad and helpful:

"The archetypal idea of "home" points in two directions at once. It points backward toward

2 Another often-cited concept in spirituality circles is "taking a long, loving look at the real."

an original hint and taste for union, starting in the body of our mother. We all came from some sort of home, even a bad one that always plants a seed of a possible and ideal paradise. And it points us forward, urging us toward the realization that this taste of union might actually be true. It guides us like an inner compass or a "homing" device... Most of us cannot let go of this implanted promise...It calls us both backward and forward, to our foundation and our future, at the same time."[8]

How we hold our personal idea of "home" is vitally important to a congruent Self; a Self that has the strongest sense of integrity and wholeness.

Diverse Wisdom teachers suggest our first home is within mothers; the second is external to us as we search, discover, and wander. The final is a return to a renewed sense of home, and to the physical community setting where we're most deeply called.

Home becomes an experience of our authentic Self within the dynamics of the intimate and larger community. It is the home we always knew as home, but is also home again, for the first time.[3]

Without his honestly painful struggle with depression, Parker Palmer wouldn't have left his confining life. Without wrestling with her struggles

---

3 T.S. Eliot, "And the end of all our exploring; Will be to arrive where we started; And know the place for the first time." *Four Quartets*

over raising Adam, Martha Beck wouldn't have the substance, the tested mettle she offers, even as her relatively young journey continues.

Paying deliberate attention to the journey shows us the brilliance of our humanity. And then, with tender vulnerability, we can offer authentic compassion to others we encourage to imagine that they, too, can heal and grow.

Without struggle, without the whole journey, we observe life from increasingly irrelevant ivory towers. But instead, through embracing the honest messiness of it all to be able to say, "I wouldn't (couldn't) change a thing," is the height of redeemed self-aware humility.

As if by magic, our personal growth opens the way to acceptance and forgiveness of everyone else, too.

Within the healing journey of reclaiming true Self, we discover empowerment, personal freedom, and Beloved Community. When we embrace the whole of our human journey, we will finally know the safe place within that is home.

CHAPTER THREE
(RE)DISCOVERING TRUE SELF

"The purpose of kneading is to make sure the clay has smooth consistency. When it is cut through, air pockets or hard lumps should reveal themselves."[9]

After forming a morning's worth of clay, the potter selects the first lump to shape into a bowl.

Different clay body's composition, which makes up its various attributes, becomes more obvious as the mud-to-masterpiece process goes along. Present or absent minerals, especially iron, interacting with various glazes that are applied and then "fired" onto the clay, will act in highly distinctive ways.

"Factory produced" ceramic items appear to be all alike. That is an aim. But the greater value of ceramic art lies in permitting the inherent makeup of the clay to come through in ways the experienced artist can emphasize.

Like all of us, this unique bit of clay has been on a long journey.

So the clay is kneaded like bread dough, and then sliced through to find air pockets that could damage or destroy a piece in kiln firing which climbs to over 2,000 degrees. And after the slicing to find air pockets, it's kneaded again before the transformation into art.

This careful process includes a "trial by fire," as the oven's heat reveals the truth hidden within a seemingly perfectly constructed clay sculpture. The "necessary suffering" a clay body goes through prepares it for the kiln, and the best possible result for the invested time and energy.

And Buddhists suggest that it is through non-resistance to suffering, seeing that it's a natural part of life's journey, we might fully wake up to our lives.

So, I invite you to imagine clay preparation as metaphor for how we discover "of what we are really made;" noticing the value of our kneading, slicing, and rekneading experiences as various important teachers we could have missed or misunderstood while growing up.

Some of us, in being kneaded and formed, were treated thoughtfully, slowly, even gently. Respect was paid, by parents and teachers, to the fact that we needed to be called out into the world: That souls are shy.

But some potters prepare clay by slamming it around, too. They drop the whole 25 pound bag to the ground to begin eliminating unwanted air bubbles and redistributing moisture. They are vigorous, and seem to just want to get through this phase in handling unformed clay so that they can get to doing art.

But, we now realize that the "art part" actually begins with appreciating the makeup of the clay itself, what it is made of before we touch it, and then handling it more appreciatively and appropriately: There will be a better result.

As with lumps of pliable clay, we tend to decide what we'd like for our children before they reveal who they are to us. Many assumptions were made about us, even before we were born. Waiting patiently for something or someone to simply show up, without developing our own expectations, is a rare human gift. So, we spend the rest of our lives uncovering and reclaiming the truth of our perfection at birth.[4]

The unfortunate usual expression is, "We become whom we were born to be." But, the clearer concept is more likely that we originally arrived as our Self. On first blush, it may seem a subtle difference, but it has dramatic consequences if instead of beholding a perfect newborn being, we unfortunately assume we are holding a baby who will *eventually become* someone.

Like kneading and slicing, life experience reveals the strengths and tender places in our Self. And as Life works with us, as our life is carved and decorated through pleasures and pains, we take on the unique attributes of our individuality, and are finally fired with colorful glazes. So at last, after all is said and done, we are revealed as the priceless masterpieces we've always been.

But how do we uncover and claim the beauty of True Self? You know, the wonderful little child who was content to simply sit and play for hours and hours? How do we rediscover our True Self after all these miles and years of detours and adventure?

---

4 Both Alice Miller, M.D., and John Bradshaw, Ph.D., have published astounding and practical insights into reclaiming and healing our own wise and creative child. Their education and experience offers second chances at the fullness of life in the second half of life.

It appears to take both a willingness to imagine a distinctly fresh perspective and then our deep commitment to personal healing and wholeness.[5]

In helping answer our questions about the process of unearthing True Self, Richard Rohr is as verbally direct as the idea of kneading and slicing clay: "Your True Self is who you objectively are from the beginning, in the mind and heart of God, "the face you had before you were born," as the Zen masters say. It is your substantial self, your absolute identity, which can be neither gained nor lost by any technique, group affiliation, morality, or formula whatsoever."[10]

Brother Richard continues:

"(T)here is necessary suffering that cannot be avoided, which Jesus calls "losing our very life," or losing what I and others call the "false self." Your false self is your role, title, and personal image that is largely a creation of your own mind and attachments. It will and must die in exact correlation to how much you want the Real. "How much false self are you willing to shed to find your True Self?" is the lasting question. Such necessary suffering will always feel like dying...If your spiritual guides do not talk to you about dying, they are not good spiritual guides!"[11]

---

5 See the illuminating exercises in *Homecoming: Reclaiming and Championing Your Inner Child* by John Bradshaw.

This personal commitment of embracing our unavoidable, "necessary," suffering will be explored further in chapter five. But for now, as we recover True Self, we have an opportunity to go beyond merely living out our lives. We have the renewed opportunity to be fully alive in the daily celebration of Life itself.

An extraordinary educator and spiritual mentor, Parker Palmer's unvarnished honesty set me on my deep journey to authenticity even before I was ready to fully commit to True Self. It was an academic trip long before it made its way to the place into which Truth has to finally drop: the heart.

In A Hidden Wholeness, Palmer offers these hard-won observations:

"In sixty-five years on earth, my pattern has never been onward and upward. It has always been up and down and back around. I follow the thread of true self faithfully for awhile. Then I lose it and find myself back in the dark, where fear drives me to search for the thread once again. That pattern, as far as I can tell, is inherent in the human condition."[12]

And Palmer continues with the soundest way to approach this intimate and delicate work with gentle friends:

"The facilitator guides by means of a poem, a story, a piece of music, or a work of art---any metaphorical embodiment that allows us to approach the topic (of rediscovering True Self) indirectly...For a while, it may sound as if we are talking about the poet's journey toward selfhood. But we soon come to understand that whatever we say about the poem, we are saying about ourselves...by addressing (True Selfhood) via a poem, we can hold it at whatever distance we choose while staying focused on meaningful matters...we develop the trust to speak more directly about ourselves. The shy soul emerges more frequently and needs less protective cover to speak."[13]

There is power in the simplicity of using art, (in our case ceramics,)to do the gentle prodding, the initial thawing, that is often needed in giving ourselves permission to dare risking what we'll find when we explore the deepest mystery on earth: our own Selves.

It's interesting that, in order to reclaim the fullness of the beauty of who we deeply are, it might become an excavation project of nearly mammoth proportions. The labor-intensive process, the drilling down through years of self-protecting layers, takes intentional, clear-eyed commitment.[6]

---

6 Intentionally selecting marble blocks from the quarry, reportedly, Michelangelo would "see" the masterpiece within it that he would "release" through his sculpting genius.

Thomas Merton, the ever-popular mystic who died relatively young at age 53 in 1968, owned an uncanny wisdom about human beings. Drawn from a full life before becoming a Trappist monk, he still speaks to us as a contemporary. Merton offered this thought from *New Seeds of Contemplation*:

"True inner self must be drawn up like a jewel from the bottom of the sea, rescued from confusion, from indiscretion, from immersion in the common, the nondescript, the trivial, the sordid, the evanescent."[14] [7]

In each case, Rohr, Palmer, and Merton all indicate a rather drastic effort is required to rediscover the sacred Self that is us. This implies something important: *That it takes a concerted sociopsychological-cultural effort to bury, disguise, and compromise our True Self in the first place.*

Why do well-intentioned parents and teachers, generation after generation, work so hard to recreate and control perfect Selves into socially appropriate children at the incalculable expense of their true Selves? This is the question at the heart of the work of brilliant child psychotherapist, Alice Miller.[8]

---

7 Evanescence: *American Heritage Dictionary*, "To dissipate or disappear like vapor."

8 Author of *The Drama of the Gifted Child*, in a dozen books Dr. Miller gave voice to the powerless, and asked some of the most difficult questions about unexamined child-rearing practices, including WWII Germany.

The precisely right underlying issue is necessary in order to discuss a way forward. And all the literature points us to generalized and unexamined fear.

When we believe we should be afraid of something or someone, we go to extraordinary lengths to calm and protect ourselves. Unexamined, unqualified, and unfocused fears can grow to impossible-to-manage proportions, and our efforts to remedy this disquiet can range from mild to extreme, from intelligent to certifiably insane.

Parents everywhere are heard lamenting, "My children are driving me crazy. I don't know what to do with them." Mystifying and challenging children become things requiring control.

If we do not take time to acknowledge our specified feelings, fear can then hover like a vague but thick fog in and around everything we do and think about. Generalized helplessness gets reinforced.

So, perhaps the exercise for the new millennium can be for us to ask ourselves specifically: *"Right now, of what am I really so afraid?"*

Both spiritual maturity and intelligent courage are required to address our fears. Fear, an emotion, cannot be well-examined and resolved only out of our emotions. For reasons that can be thoroughly explained through volumes of outstanding

25

modern psycho-biological research, a rational mind and matured heart must intentionally intervene in near-instinctual-level fear responses.

In everyday life, though, we don't often momentarily stop to bring our faculties to bear on everyday discomforts, and so add yet another layer to our generalized sense of social isolation and personal confusion. So then, it becomes even more work for us to locate and draw up, to rescue, that precious jewel that we all are, from the depths of the sea.

Popular Buddhist nun, Pema Chodron, shares pithy wisdom in ways North Americans can easily absorb. Pema offers another metaphor that might make the point if our previous mentors haven't quite struck the chord:

"When you leave the cradle of loving kindness, you are in this beautiful suit of armor that you might have had some illusion was protecting you from something, only to find that actually it's shielding you from being fully alive and fully awake. Then you go forward and you meet the dragon, and every meeting shows you where there's still some armor to take off...That's what we're doing here, removing armor, removing our protections, undoing all the stuff that covers our wisdom and our gentleness and our awake quality. We're not trying to be something we aren't; rather we're rediscovering, reconnecting with who we are. I am awake; I will spend the rest of my life taking my armor off."[15]

We are being introduced to the liberating and mysterious idea of paradox: living with an *apparent* opposition between two things like good and evil, or scarcity and abundance or the individual and the community, even death and resurrection.

How is it that facing our dragons can be the very arena within which our sophisticated self-protective armor is dissolved and a true heart revealed? How is it that all the logic in the world falls apart when it comes to maturing into the fullness of whom we truly are?

This is the mysterious, powerful brilliance of paradox: a statement that seems to contradict common sense and yet is perhaps true.

Pema shows us the humor that often comes from paradox,

"When you just get flying and all feels so good and you think, "This is it, this is the path that has heart," you suddenly fall flat on your face. Everybody's looking at you. You say to yourself, "What happened to that path that had heart? This feels like the path full of mud in my face." It's like someone laughing in your ear, challenging you to figure out what to do when you don't know what to do. It humbles you. It opens your heart."[16]

27

The next chapter, in part by means of paradox, takes us directly into a confrontation of fear. And how it becomes the source, then, of freedom.

CHAPTER FOUR
FREEDOM AND FEAR

"A beginner...who cannot center the clay without help is in a hopeless position; left alone, he or she can do nothing at all. The difficulty of centering clay probably accounts for more despair and disillusion among beginners than anything else."[17]

An experienced potter knows the exact pressure and amount of water needed to center clay on the spinning wheel and begin well.

The ceramics metaphor continues to be especially helpful by offering the Wisdom of being well-centered within True Self, so we can savor Life's entire ride.

When we stand with a sense of both feet planted on solid ground, we are centered in our place, our home in the world, and can then afford to look at Life's possibilities with matured eyes, wide open.

Only when we are metaphorically planted can we paradoxically run with joy.

This chapter's heading, "Freedom *and* Fear," was not the initial title. The original was the more commonly understood: "Freedom *from* Fear." But, after study, reflection, and rethinking definitions of fear, there's an opportunity to reconsider how freedom *and fear* effectively coexist. Fear is revitalizing, if we'll courageously welcome such a possibility.

Freedom *and* fear is another great paradox.

Fearlessness is not, as it turns out, the same thing as being courageous. Courage is the "mental or moral strength to *venture, persevere, and withstand* danger, fear, or difficulty." Its origin is from the old French for "heart."

To be courageous is to acknowledge our fears and intentionally live with them, through them. But, interestingly, "bravery" and "valor" stress a "bold and daring *defiance* of danger."[18] And I think this important difference is where we have space to grow our further understanding of being more fully equipped to live and flourish.

So, why focus our attention on *developing moral courage to persevere* when confronted with fear, *rather than boldly defy* it? There are two important elements here: 1) We seldom take the time to carefully name and understand to what we are reacting, and; 2) We don't appreciate how fears might actually function.

The fuller dictionary definition for "fear" is not widely known. And knowing what fear is takes us a long way toward seeing what it offers. Like so many strange and unfamiliar giants in fairy tales, and the innocent little children who meet them, we also might befriend our oversized fears, real and imagined, and become people of great courage.

Fear is defined by *Webster's* as, "1: an unpleasant often strong emotion caused by expectation or awareness of danger 2: anxious concern: worry 3: reverential awe especially toward God. – Syn: FEAR is the general term and implies great anxiety and usually loss of courage."[19]

Notice the third definition of fear is where our unexplored possibilities lie: fear as "reverential awe" with regard to the mysterious, unknown, and the especially uncontrollable things in life. We can decide to do nothing but simply notice that we are afraid. We are experiencing the awe of encountering a mystery.

Pema Chodron offers this paradox about fear of uncontrollable things: "There's a sense of freedom when we accept that we're not in control. Pointing ourselves toward what we would most like to avoid makes our barriers and shields permeable. This may lead to a don't-know-what-to-do kind of feeling."[20]

She continues with specifics, saying we *especially* notice this in-between lostness when things are falling apart. "If we've just learned that we have cancer...If someone we love just died or walked out, the outer places we go for comfort feel feeble and ephemeral."[21] [9]

Like not-quite-centered clay on the potter's wheel, when confronted with Uncontrollable Mystery, we lose our equilibrium and know we are in danger of shooting right off the wheel (and, in our unexamined terror, *shoot into oblivion*, which is impossible, as your rational mind well knows.)

When confronted by death or debilitating illnesses, we go all wobbly. And that makes sense on many levels. But that doesn't mean we need to stay afraid and incapacitated. Our grief need not become an alibi to do nothing. And just as important, it also doesn't mean we need to try to

---

9 Ephemeral means to "last only a day; a very short time."

ruthlessly rush back to our previously familiar "normal."

Our previous "normal" is permanently altered whether we embrace it as true or not. This is priceless wisdom from Pema and counter-cultural to those who don't make time to treat their lives with reverential awe:

"Anxiety, heartbreak, and tenderness mark the in-between-state. It's the kind of place we usually want to avoid. The challenge is to stay in the middle rather than to buy into struggle and complaint. The challenge is to let it soften us rather than make us more rigid and afraid... When we are brave enough to stay in the middle of nowhere, compassion arises spontaneously. By not knowing, not hoping to know, and not acting like we know what's happening, we begin to access our inner strength...The fact is that we spend a long time in the middle...Resting here completely---steadfastly experiencing the clarity of the present moment—is called enlightenment."[22]

It takes *more* courage to feel our confused feelings around shocking diagnoses or loss than to dismiss them and instead put on a "brave face." Remember the definition of bravery is *defiance* of danger or fear. And when we fail to realize the wall we're erecting against so much initially undefined pain, we are starting down a road where our armor will create internal divisions and separation from others.

Instead of simply stopping and holding our overwhelming sea of grief and honoring the truth of what has come in to change our lives forever, we move away from the naturally brilliant ability we have to come to know what we are feeling, and what impact it is beginning to have in making us more fully human and interconnected.

I made this unconscious choice over and over as a young adult. Others marveled at my "inner strength." They should have wondered how I could bury all those people before I was 30 and make it look so easy. But no one ever asked; and I never imagined I owed my lost loved ones, and my own broken heart, even a few days of deep grieving to acknowledge I was utterly shaken and lost. For years I buried myself in work and schooling.

I might have been terrorized at the thought of acknowledging that much suffering. But, I didn't realize I'd missed an opportunity to enter into the deepest Mystery of Life and Life after physical death. I missed out on exercising the definition of fear that involves respectful awe.

Like so many, I thought I could skip the messiness and despair of Life's necessary suffering by ignoring it. Ironically, the suffering became layered and complicated, and was prolonged.

Our culture tries to ignore what we fear most, and with great consequence. We react to the "unthinkable" by awkwardly denying it and then anesthetizing ourselves in myriad ways.

The recent near-global economic depression was fraught with declarations that behemoth institutions were "too big to fail." So we loosened regulations that had ensured we looked carefully at what we were actually doing.

Families with histories of serious health concerns have members who would "rather not know" and avoid annual check- ups. And we eat-on-the-run and refuse to incorporate regular exercise, acting as if we are robots who live to work instead of people who work as part of living.

We do this all without thinking. And so, keep our eyes firmly shut.

The PTSD sufferers among our service members, from repeated deployments to witness or participate in unspeakable violence, are returning to us with spirits screaming in pain. Paradoxically, these brave and deeply wounded warriors can be the very teachers we've needed to soften our dysfunctional cultural conditioning to simply "move on" after hearing of natural disasters, divorces, and deaths of dearest loved ones.

From more recent and healthier personal experience, and many wise mentors referenced in these pages, I'm sure we can choose to mindfully experience freedom in and through fear. Because it's not the already gentle giants in life, the easy people and happy experiences, who enrich us the most; it's the fierce and fiery dragon, in the form of illness or challenging person who, astonishingly, becomes gentle through the development of respect for our own courageous compassion.

It's a paradox: it defies logic to trust fear and pain to teach us and set us free.

Pema pithily summarizes how limited perspectives sabotage spiritual and social maturation and freedom:

"We suffer when we resist the noble and irrefutable truth of impermanence and death...First, we expect that what is always changing should be graspable and predictable...and we suffer. Second, we proceed as if we were separate from everything else. We mistake the openness of our being---the inherent wonder and surprise of each moment---for a solid, irrefutable self. Third, we look for happiness in all the wrong places. In repeating our quest for instant gratification, pursuing addictions of all kinds---we strengthen dysfunctional patterns. Thus we become less and less able to reside with even the most fleeting uneasiness or discomfort. We can stop harming ourselves and others in our efforts to escape the alternation of pleasure and pain. We can relax and be fully present for our lives." [23]

We have nearly finished drilling to the bottom of this cold and creaky mine and have probably hit pay dirt: The word that may best capture the heart of our deepest fear is the word "suffering."

Mentally healthy people do not heartily welcome pain and suffering. But they recognize and appropriately deal with it when it shows up. And here is a stunning and important paradox on this very issue: Richard Rohr cites brilliant pioneer psychologist Carl Jung who echoes other Wisdom teachers:

"Carl Jung said so much unnecessary suffering comes into the world because people will not accept the "legitimate suffering" that comes from being human. In fact, he said neurotic behavior is usually the result of refusing that legitimate suffering! Ironically, this refusal of the necessary pain of being human brings to the person ten times more suffering in the long run... Before the truth sets you free, it tends to make you miserable."[24]

After doing the deep and very messy work of watching my own fiery dragons become gentle teachers, like you, I can attest to the reality that before the truth sets us free, it most likely will make us absolutely miserable!

As we journey on, we'll better grasp how thoughtfully naming and tenderly facing our fears, approaching what scares us with respectful awe, makes dragon-tamers of us all.

CHAPTER FIVE

RAINS FALL AND THE SUN SHINES ON EVERYONE

"No other material on Earth undergoes such dramatic transformation as clay through fire. Most materials on Earth are obliterated by high heat...In order for ceramic wares to be strong and durable, they must be fired to maturation."[25]

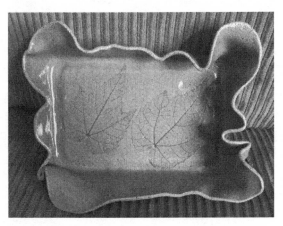

Porcelain free-form dish by the author

Surrendering a degree of artistic control, the clay was allowed to slump into the form and respond freely.

Many ceramicists prefer an approach called "hand building." The clay is rolled out and the artist forms what she likes without the aid of a potter's wheel. Sometimes it's freestanding and other times forms are used, against which the clay rests and shapes itself as it dries.

Like a thin sheet of pie dough, the artist lays the clay across another form, seeing how the clay folds itself into or over it. It always lends elements of surprise.

Sometimes the surprises, after glazing and firing, are utterly delightful. Other times, the results are simply mystifying.

The sun shines and the rain falls on everyone, Jesus said. On both the "just and the unjust." Things will happen. But we have a funny way of emphasizing what's highlighted for us in unfiltered, busy moments. It's a matter of what gets our attention.

Rainy or stormy days tend to hold our attention more successfully than do sunny ones. Things that cause us worry or inconvenience are brighter on our radar than cool and gentle streams of water that also permeate everyday life.

It's part of self-preservation biology.

With that predisposition in mind, another helpful fable illustrates how we can mindfully and deliberately *choose* to see things more broadly; it is called *The Taoist Farmer*:

"A farmer had only one horse, and one day the horse ran away. The neighbors came to console over his terrible loss. The farmer said, "What makes you think it is so terrible?"

A month later, the horse came home–this time bringing with her two beautiful wild horses. The neighbors became excited at the farmer's good fortune. Such lovely strong horses! The farmer said, "What makes you think this is good fortune?"

The farmer's son was thrown from one of the wild horses and broke his leg. All the neighbors were very distressed. Such bad luck! The farmer said, "What makes you think it is bad?"

A war came, and every able-bodied man was conscripted and sent into battle. Only the farmer's son, because he had a broken leg, remained. The neighbors congratulated the farmer. "What makes you think this is good?" said the farmer.

The point of the story here is not to frame daily events in one's life in terms of good or bad, but dispassionately. You never know when or how fortune will shine or cast a shadow on you. We can't always assume what seems good or lucky will wind up having only positive effects.

In other words, we can't always know how a current event will eventually shake out. Some versions of this fable continue with the spared young man becoming despondent and causing mayhem to the people of his village.

Deciding an event in our lives is a good or bad thing may be premature judgment, and that is wisdom worth holding as we mature and grow.

You have personal examples of many times you were distressed at a plan being delayed or cancelled, only to discover it was a blessing that it was postponed or ended. Or a relationship you "just knew" was meant to be a pivotal, lifetime connection...isn't (at least, not so far.) And how very much that hurt at the time, and perhaps for years afterward.

But today you can remember, and breathe a sigh of relief that you forgave yourself, the other person, even Life itself, and gave yourself permission to keep putting one foot in front of the other.

And now, despite those initial hurts and fears, here you are.

This is the refining fire, the previously mentioned "necessary suffering," as many traditions call it, that draws out purest Self. Our Self is ours for the uncovering and rediscovering, and it requires intentionality. This is the truth of Life that is not popular in North American culture, where we prefer the pursuit of happiness and living happily ever after. We buy myriad insurance policies hoping to ward off consequences of our everyday bumps, breaks, and bruises.

The goal of every parent I've ever met was to have happy children. Without exception: Happy children. What a grand-scale set up for everyone involved (but most excellent for the advertising industry.)

In our ruggedly individualistic society, the idea of opening ourselves to the possibility we should sit still with the pain of our discomforts and sadnesses rather than run or medicate them away is counter-culture thinking. Tragically, it is spiritually costly for us to avoid the unexpected benefits of deeply sitting with hurt and confusion, as it often leads to compassionate loving kindness for ourselves and others.

But, like the profound discomfort of ice packs placed on injured limbs, we have to be willing to get past the initial sting and reflexive response to throw them off so the healing relief can show up for us. And when the wounded area is calmed, we are better able to see the big picture and relax in tending better to our injury, and perhaps, even learning what it might teach us.

Pema Chodron speaks to this instinctual preference to shut our eyes rather than "see clearly what is, with gentleness":

"Instead there's a kind of basic misunderstanding that we should try to be better than we already are, that we should try to improve ourselves, that we should try to get away from painful things, and that if we could just learn how to get away from painful things, then we would be happy. That is the innocent, naïve misunderstanding that we all share, which keeps us unhappy... The problem is the desire to change is fundamentally a form of aggression toward yourself...Our neurosis and our wisdom is made out of the same material. If you throw out your neurosis, you also throw out your wisdom."[26]

Read this next wisdom carefully, especially if this degree of self-acceptance is too hard to imagine:

"The idea isn't to try to get rid of your anger, but to make friends with it, to see it clearly with precision and honesty, and also see it with gentleness....It involves learning how, once you have fully acknowledged the feeling of anger and the knowledge of who you are and what you do, to let it go."[27]

As I've experienced our culture, there is little-to-no tolerance for human feelings in the workplace. So, unsuccessfully, we swallow our responses to daily events. But our feelings are real; we cannot possibly repress them forever.

Unexamined feelings will act on us because they seem true.

Growing up, many of us heard we were "too sensitive." That somehow, we should simply stop feeling. Didn't you wonder what you should do with your intuitions, and feelings in general, in order to make others more comfortable?

Our various work environments require us to be unemotional. We are to look "put together" from the outside. And thanks to a lot of physical exercise, for awhile we might keep our blood pressure at acceptable levels; but deep inside we're still responding to every nuance in our interactions.

Like many of us, after years passed and I had objective distance from several antiseptic institutions, I was angry at how compliant I'd been. I resented the human cost to everyone who is compelled to repress responses to injustices and slights to ourselves or others.

But, here's an insight that helped me forgive those who actively sought to reform my intuitive nature. In understanding the social dynamic that's at work, perhaps it can unlock years of resentment for you, too:

"Resentment is the *anger* you feel when you think someone has victimized you... But, our injuries from others often result from their need to take care of themselves, *rather than their desire to hurt us.* Such people *are not aware* that they may be taking care of themselves *offensively and inappropriately.* But we, in our immature way of thinking, believe *they are aware* and that *they have deliberately set out to hurt us*...we (finally) understand that much of the time they are actually attempting (only) to take care of themselves."[28]

Perhaps one of the strangest and most helpful insights we might receive is, "It's not about you." Most people who hurt us are not even seeing us. Their untoward behavior or words do not come from a compassionate place for you or for themselves. Defensive responses come from thoughtless places of fear, resulting in the ongoing and mindless exercise of adding additional layers to their self-protecting armor.

The ability to grasp this wisdom within the real time of a hurtful moment is owning mindfulness: the ability to see with our eyes wide open.

Mindfulness is an ongoing practice that requires mature discipline and intentional awareness. It requires we become fully present throughout the day. Every wisdom tradition teaches that seeing with eyes wide open is at the very heart of developing loving-kindness and compassion for ourselves and every living thing.

Some traditions call it "enlightenment," others term it "Christ-consciousness."

And if we have the self-awareness to see the pattern that the tapestry of our individual lives is in the process of weaving, that the colors are rich with the bumps and triumphs, breaks and healings, bruises and restorations, stormy moments and so very many sunny days.

Without the colorful richness of the unpredictable journey involved in uncovering our True Selves, we could just as well be one vast sea of beige.

Speaking of tapestry, wise teachers have asked us to look at the other side of these amazing, painstaking works of art. Looking on the backside, the part purposely turned over to reveal the intentional, planned, breathtakingly beautiful side, is instructive.

In studying the messy parts that support the art, we realize that without the knots and stray threads, there could be no priceless masterpiece that has stood the test of time and style.

By this point in our journey together, I hope our stubbornly-held cultural assumption that good (enough) lives should be nothing but happiness, sounds more and more hollow. That a life free of inconvenience, illness, or sadnesses now seems vulgar, meaning it lacks a depth and richness of matured perception.

We cannot have priceless works of art, including you and me, without the messy ceramics studio or the reverse side of handiwork. It all, necessarily, goes together.

The following account is an example of sitting with suffering instead of running away. In receiving permission to tell our story, she said that helping someone else would be a wonderful thing to try to do.

Because I'd experienced or witnessed first-hand suffering akin to my friend's loss, she believed I might be of pastoral use. And though a wildly successful leader and mentor, the roles she most cherishes remain that of being a wife and mother.

As with so very many talented young people, my friend's youngest adult daughter struggled with depression and was stubborn about taking her prescribed medication. And one day, despite her family's unconditional and very present love and support, after an argument with a friend, she took her own life.

In the many months since this life-altering moment, I've witnessed the most astonishingly authentic and brutally honest questions about what my faithful friend had assumed about her contract with God. And with Life itself.

This event was simply unacceptable.

As a new mother, my friend had told God she would do absolutely everything good for others; be utterly selfless in the face of the most outrageous expectations, always and everywhere, with only one condition: God would look after her children and always keep them safe from harm.

So when she lost her youngest, despite the constant and nearby presence of family members, my friend was undone.

I recognized her agonizing questions as they came up. I knew how badly her abdomen ached from perpetual, anguished crying.

After walking with my friend to her deepest and most emotionally wrenching places, on my own, I journeyed back to do even deeper personal grieving. I'd settled, like most Americans who seek psychotherapy, only for "talking it out." Called "cognitive therapy," it's efficient and appropriate for some circumstances, but doesn't generally get past our reasonable-linguistic-brain to the emotional center.

Cognitive therapy might help us understand reasons for things: why it hurt, and why we did such-and-thus in response. But we don't get to the reservoir of deepest feelings without a deliberate intention to get there, and usually with a brave and competent healing partner.

As mentioned earlier, clay has "memory." And many of us experience chronic aches, pains and illnesses, like some allergies and auto-immune disorders, because our clay, our body, remembers and stores our ungrieved woundedness. It sits, stored and agitated. It waits to be fully and respectfully acknowledged.

If we don't make time to listen to our uncried tears, seek to deepen compassion for ourselves and others, we cannot fully heal. We cannot grow. Period.

Because my friend had the courage to work deeply and go "all the way down," I was gifted to discover a new level of personal healing, as the salve of compassion for my friend and myself washed over us. This is an example of what Henri Nouwen described as the purpose for his own life as a "wounded healer." We cannot help others heal if we do not authentically face our own deep suffering.

We've been culturally lulled into believing we can create a perfectly safe and sanitary life. That good boys and girls have uneventful, linear tracks toward "success," all the way to the top of their field. And it's simply not true.

The truth is, the sun shines and rains fall and things happen: to everyone.

Wrong-headed culturally-based and media-reinforced expectations set us up to doubt the Creator's love for us, and reduce our opportunity to be fully alive to the truth of our precious lives, messy choices and consequences and all.

And something important is steadily emerging for my friend. Something that helps her imagine the possibility that her daughter's choice that afternoon had nothing to do with my friend being a not-good-enough mother or God looking the other way. There was something that made sense when nothing else possibly could: Free will.

My friend's beautiful daughter flatly refused to take medication that could have relieved the penetrating sadness her brain chemistry foisted on her moods. She didn't want to accept and work through her medical condition.

As a young and independent adult, she exercised her free will. And that freedom is paramount to the understanding of our agency in our own lives to which my friend ascribes. With all of life's complications and consequences of natural events beyond our control, we still have the freedom to choose what we will do; to *choose how we will respond*, to events in our lives.

Gradually imagining, over our months of talks, her daughter as a young adult with choices of her own, rather than a still-dependent child, was part of the fundamental shifting my friend had to do. Many parents never make that liberating adjustment.

And once she was able to hold her daughter's autonomy with mutuality and respect, it became possible that a thoughtless God wasn't controlling the strings of her daughter's life. Rather, her daughter made a deliberate choice that later yielded unspeakably tragic consequences in a single, fateful, moment of despair.

And though life is holding brightness and many new joys, every day my friend misses her daughter. The stray threads and knots will always be tangible on the backside of her brilliant tapestry, holding her priceless artwork together.

This difficult story is offered as one glimpse into what healing might be possible around our deepest wounding. Because we all hold painful memories, we can mindfully seek the courage to begin setting ourselves free.

Who is the wounded healer in your life? The therapist, pastor, or friend, aunt, uncle, grandparent or cousin? Who is the safe person with whom you might deliberately journey and rediscover the uncried tears your body remembers, so you can be well and truly free?

Your priceless vessel, your brilliant tapestry, is waiting for your full embrace.

CHAPTER SIX
SECRET TO DEEP PEACE: "DYING" BEFORE YOU DIE

"Raku (clay firing method) means "happiness through chance," and…modern techniques have now removed much of the chance, though results are still unpredictable and losses are high."[29]

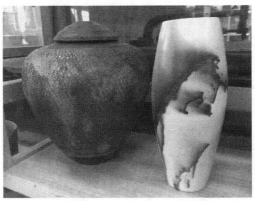

Raku pots by Laura Rose

Some artists make the free fall into the uncontrollable unknown of Raku firing look so easy, often with extraordinarily stunning results.

A Raku artist is a gutsy potter. After creating remarkable ceramic pieces and painting them with specific glazes, they intentionally put them into a red-hot Raku kiln for an hour or so, then plunge the pottery into a metal waste can filled with newspapers that dramatically catch fire and burn ash all around their vulnerably glazed pieces.

Some of the most stunningly marvelous surprises come from this firing method. On the other hand, if the artist had a specific outcome in mind, they experience some of their biggest disappointments. The Raku method is simply impossible to perfectly control.

The experienced potter accepts this element of unknowing, and proceeds into the adventure with their eyes wide open: The thrill of letting go of personal expectations is worth the risk. Whatever happens will happen.

In a sort of parallel thought pattern, in this chapter several poignant elders describe how, if we work to come to terms with dying before we expect to die, we can know deep peace. And, it seems fair to say, our personal peace could well gravitate out to impact the rest of the world, too.

Through several "near death" experiences in my youth, I had the early opportunity to notice that life-threatening experiences can be surprising.[10] However, letting go of people we love is, somehow, something very different from imaging our own physical death. Separations from loved ones through death hurt: human suffering hurts.

"Dying before we die," involves going even deeper. And since we've spoken about the vital importance of recovering our "good enough" True Self, and discussed freedom and fear co-existing, this might be a good place to consider dying before we die.

We've traveled the preliminary ground in order to be able to go into the most important issue North Americans tend to refuse to face, much less discuss. But if we'd risk looking, our lives could be radically energized and spiritually clarified.

Diverse sages teach that this part of our human reality is worth our earliest possible consideration. When we've better confronted and relinquished the generalized sense of "death's grip on our lives," spiritually speaking, we back away from teetering in undifferentiated terror over the edge of a cliff that drops into an unknown abyss. Instead, we live and breathe deeply into the fullness of rich and colorful lives.

---

10 You probably have your own near-death memory. (Many death-defying stories involve being in automobiles while impaired and/or distracted.) Take a moment here to consider: Have those events made a difference in your life? Have there been spiritual gifts out of those experiences?

We can *decide* to be wide awake and grateful on a level we've never imagined. In choosing greater understanding and compassion, there can be a lifetime of deep peace and gratitude.

Life is precious and death is, as Pema Chodron's said, "a noble and irrefutable truth." We will die. People we cannot imagine living without, will die. And nobody I know is very happy about it. But socio-culturally, we can think about our physical passing much better than we currently do.

Since the beginning of recorded history, we know Wisdom teachers have tried addressing anxious people's persistent concerns over death in general, as well as the heartbreaking question, "What happens when I die?"

A relatively new Wisdom teacher is Cynthia Bourgeault. Along with Elaine Pagels[11], she's introducing many to the Gnostic Gospels (accounts of Jesus of Nazareth not chosen for inclusion in *The Bible*) in a gentle and thoughtful manner. And in her little book, *Mystical Hope*, she has this to say about dying before you die:

"In Tolstoy's great novella *The Death of Ivan Ilych*, he describes how Ivan, down to the final days of his life, screaming and struggling against going into what he perceives to be the "black sack" of his death, suddenly experiences a shift

---

11 For more, please see Dr. Pagel's highly acclaimed *The Gnostic Gospels*.

like the sensation one sometimes experiences in a railway carriage when one thinks one is going backward while one is really going forward and suddenly becomes aware of the real direction... In place of death there was light. "So that's what it is!" He suddenly exclaimed aloud, "What joy!"

To a few of the truly spiritually courageous it has seemed, then, that the real trick would be to end the resistance—go through the inner shift of direction—*before* the end of one's actual physical life. The practice is called "dying before you die," and it represents the highest aspiration of all the spiritual paths. "For the mystery is this, explains Rumi: that the gifts come after you die and not before." Only after the terror of one's own diminishment and annihilation, after the last scraps of clinging to life at any cost have been left behind forever, is it possible to truly live in hope." [30]

It fascinates, that rather than this release of control leading to our becoming dismally resigned to whatever happens to us, we actually feel such freedom that we are more empowered and energized; we have hope.

Time magazine reported that Steve Job's final words were, "Oh, wow! Oh, wow! Oh, wow!" And one day we'll be able to "see" what images are registering in people's minds, but for now, it seems Mr. Jobs might have witnessed something utterly amazing as he was letting go of his physical life.

Death is still an amazing mystery, even for a great wizard of our generation.

In *Doing Nothing,* Steven Harrison asks us to question our assumptions as he lays out a brief run-down of how we "got here," in our arguably limited thinking about Life:

"Newtonian physics, and its inherent materialism, was a wrong turn that took 300 years to discover. In those centuries, the Newtonian view was absorbed into our worldview. It permeated every aspect of our reality. It told us, counterintuitively, that the world was mechanical and predictable.

In those same centuries, we developed scientific principles that corresponded to this materialism. Out of this grew our medicine, our psychiatry, our view of time, aging, and ultimately death. In the Newtonian world, these are all mechanical, predictable, material.

The new paradigm of relativity and the quantum physical reality has not been absorbed. In part, it has not even been formulated by the scientists, let alone integrated by the general culture.

This new paradigm, a mutable, interconnected universe transformed by consciousness, has been realized, formulated, and expressed for thousands of years. It is the realization of mystics. It has been described in the Vedas of the Hindus, the Kabbalah of Judaism, and the teachings of the Sufis, the Christian mystics, and the Taoist sages."[31]

In this brief socio-historical recap, we again see the power of becoming what we are taught to believe since earliest schooling. It rarely occurs to us to revamp our thinking and question assumptions within the "wisdom of the day," that drastically limits what is truest for us.

Many unreasonably ascribe to the model of the self-made and completely independent individual as the highest good, as if that were even possible; at the expense of each of our fullest contribution in the nurture of human dynamics in a healthy and thriving community. More and more, science proves that we live in an interconnected universe.

Gentle spiritual teacher, Eckhart Tolle, in echoing Harrison's observations, cuts to the fundamental misunderstanding under which we, uncritically, function:

"Ego comes about through a split in the human psyche in which identity separates into two parts that we could call "I" and "me" or "me" and "myself." Every ego is therefore schizophrenic, to use the word in its popular meaning of split personality. You live with a mental image of yourself, a conceptual self that you have a relationship with. Life itself becomes conceptualized and separated from who you are when you speak of "my life." The moment you say or think "my life" and believe in what you are saying (rather than it just being a linguistic convention), you have entered into the realm of delusion. If there is such a thing as "my life," it follows that I and life are two separate things, and so I can also lose my life, my imaginary treasured possession.

Death becomes a seeming reality and a threat. Words and concepts split life into separate segments that have no reality in themselves... But how could I be separate from life? What "I" could there be apart from life, apart from Being? So there is no such thing as "my life." I *am* life.

So how could I lose my life? How can I lose something that I Am. It is impossible."[32]

When Tolle claims to be part of the capitalized "Being" and uses God's chosen name for God's self in identifying himself as "I Am," he is claiming what several traditions believe: we are made out of our Creator's essence. As Harrison told us just previously, the Wisdom teachers have been trying to let us know this, for thousands of years.

How can we, in realizing we are of an eternal Creator, ever die? Change, yes; but die? As our myriad writers all indicate: it simply isn't logical. Ultimately, it could be that the end of us we call "death," doesn't even exist.

And this "paradigm shift" as it's called, is huge. Our mental rudders can't make such a sharp turn in the heavy seas of our deepest worry over separation and loss.

But as scientists continue to explore and discover support for the physics of perpetual energy, it might not be long before we have overwhelming proof that who we ultimately are is, after all, eternal.

In the spiritual realm of discussion, it also more than makes sense. Returning to a treasured mentor, Quaker Parker Palmer offers this liberating realization from his own hard-won experience:

"Only when we lose our lives will we find them. When Jesus spoke those words, he was not exhorting people toward something they "ought" to do, but simply articulating a basic law of life. As long as we cling to life as we understand it, we cling to a pinched and deadly image of things, an image heavily conditioned by our egos, our social programming, our limited knowledge of the options. But when we are willing to let go of life as we want it to be and allow the larger reality to live in and through us instead, then in our dying we come alive.

For many of us, the life we need to lose is life lived in the image of the autonomous self, and the life we shall then find is that of the self that is embedded in community—a community that connects us not only to other people but to the natural world as well.

A culture of isolated individualism produces mass conformity because people who think they must bear life all alone are too fearful to take the risks of selfhood. But people who know that they are embedded in an eternal community are both freed and empowered to become who they were born to be."[33]

The line that best captures what I've understood from the transparent life offered by this award-winning master teacher bears repeating, *"But when we are willing to let go of life as we want it to be and allow the larger reality to live in and through us instead, then in that dying, that letting go, we come alive."*

This pearl of great price, many insist, cannot come to us in the youth of our lives; the time when we are so distracted by all the "shiny things" that whirl around and vie for our limited attention. In youth, appropriately, we are taking in information and sifting, sifting, and sifting some more.

Parker Palmer had to survive a depression so deep it's difficult to read his accounting. He was a classic academic headed toward college presidency and more. As he wrote of it, he was blindly ambitious: he never stopped to ask his soul, his True Self, what it wanted for his life.

Self-awareness came after surrendering focused energy on impressive education, credentials-getting, and professional preparations. When finally examined, his wrong-headed striving was discovered to be what it tragically was for Palmer: an exercise in perpetual, day-by-day dying of his True Self.

It is the great gift granted to the mature person, the one Brother Richard Rohr terms to be in the "second half of life," who genuinely wants their whole truth that promises to set them absolutely free.

Brother Richard ties together previous observations among our diverse Wisdom teachers,

"Every initiation rite I studied worldwide was always about "dying before you die." When you first discharge your loyal soldier, it will feel like a loss of faith or loss of self. *But it is only the death of the false self, and is often the very birth of the soul.* (Italics in original) Instead of being ego driven, you will begin to be soul drawn...No one oversees his or her own demise willingly, even when it is the false self that is dying."[34]

We see then, that a wide-awake person comes to realize, and, generally with the help of a Wisdom teacher like some you've already met, choose the authentic inner authority of internalized conscience called "soul," over the blindly obedient "loyal soldier" who is the follower of the countless socially-prescribed, but unexamined, "shoulds."

And each of us must pass through the fiery trials that test our mettle and purifies the gold we are. Each of us, if we risk leaving what is familiar and heavily reinforced to submit to the high heat required, can become something of immeasurable beauty; and a significant elder in our community.

There appears to be both "necessary suffering" and an acceptance of physical death for everyone. We cannot completely understand how or why some suffer more than others. But one thing of which I've grown certain is when we courageously seek the authenticity of our True Self, whatever suffering is in our future will be greatly mitigated. We become quicker to ask adversity, "What are you here to teach me?"

Loosening our grip, our imaginary control over our everyday physical lives, makes dying before we die possible. And inexpressible spiritual freedom has the opportunity to fill the vacuum where fear had made its home.

We have freed ourselves to come radically alive into the fullness of the beloved community.

CHAPTER SEVEN
RESURRECTION INTO BELOVED COMMUNITY

"One of the marvels of clay is its capacity to be worked and reworked until one is satisfied with the outcome...Keep a large reclaiming bucket for failed attempts...it holds moist scraps to which water and wet work are added. It can take a few days for leather-hard clay to slake down, but it will."[35]

Despite all evidence to the contrary, this recycled clay is nearly dried enough to be reformed into clay balls and thrown again into strong, useful, and beautiful pots.

It is cruel to imagine being dissolved into a "reclaiming bucket" of clay with every event termed a "failure" in our lives. Despite that, in its most vivid manifestation, incarceration seems intended as such. We are human beings and cannot be dissolved; should not be permanently isolated or "thrown away."

But like clay that's hit a major snag in its evolution toward being realized as a magnificent thing of functional beauty, we can be reconstituted; more exactly, we can be *reminded* of our True Self still being uncovered.

A following favorite story is a brilliant way of imagining approaching individuals who have forgotten whom they truly are. It's called "They're Playing Your Song" adapted from Alan Cohen, author of *Living from the Heart*:

"When a woman in a certain African tribe knows she is pregnant, she goes out into the wilderness with a few friends and together they pray and meditate until they hear the song of the child. They recognize that every soul has its own vibration that expresses its unique flavor and purpose. When the women attune to the song, they sing it out loud. Then they return to the tribe and teach it to everyone else.

When the child is born, the community gathers and sings the child's song to him or her. Later, when the child enters education, the village gathers and chants the child's song. When the child passes through the initiation to adulthood, the people again come together and sing. At the time of marriage, the person hears his or her song.

Finally, when the soul is about to pass from this world, the family and friends gather at the person's bed, just as they did at their birth, and they sing the person into the next life.

There is something inside each of us that knows we have a song, and we wish those we love would recognize it and support us to sing it. How we all long to be loved, acknowledged, and accepted for who we are.

In the African tribe there is another occasion upon which the villagers sing to the child. If at any time during his or her life, the person commits a crime or aberrant social act, the individual is called to the center of the village and the people in the community form a circle around them. Then they sing their song to them.

The tribe recognizes that the correction for antisocial behavior is not punishment; it is love and the remembrance of identity. When you recognize your own song, you have no desire or need to do anything that would hurt another.

A friend is someone who knows your song and sings it to you when you have forgotten it. Those who love you *are not fooled* by mistakes you have made or dark images you hold about yourself. They remember your beauty when you feel ugly; your wholeness when you are broken; your innocence when you feel guilty; and your purpose when you are confused.

If you do not give your song a voice, you will feel lost, alone, confused. If you express it, you will come to life. You may not have grown up in an African tribe that sings your song to you at crucial life transitions, but life is always reminding you when you are in tune with yourself and when you are not. You may feel a little warbly at the moment, but so have all the great singers. Just keep singing. You'll find your way home."

And there is an underlying assumption with this approach to bringing us back into the safe and beloved community: there must be a solid sense of trusted community within which to be nurtured.

For us to free fall into the richness of life, to take occasional risks and test prescribed boundaries as we grow, we must believe we will survive the experience. We must be able to assume that if, in fact, our initial effort was wrong-headed, we will still find welcome.[12]

We are very primal in our instinctual responses to pain and pleasure. We gravitate toward pleas-

---

12 The astonishing focus of President Nelson Mandela and Bishop Desmond Tutu, in personal and community-level reconciliation efforts at the end of South Africa's apartheid, is called the Truth and Reconciliation Commission.

ures like love and acceptance, and flee from pains like physical punishments and harsh language.

Our response to escape pain is the stronger and more rapid of the two. We react more quickly to pain avoidance. So the re-training approach called "shaping," where a behavioral scientist rewards the positive behavior they want to see whenever it appears, takes a lot longer than the apparent quick fix of punishment to "extinguish" unwanted behavior.

Loving ourselves or someone else back into True Self is a commitment of supportive moments and intimate connection. When children are surrounded by such a committed community, incarceration rates drop: We won't send our children away as if the failure is theirs alone. And a child's True Self has the safe space to notice s/he is surrounded by other True Selves.

Redemption or resurrection is what we are addressing, and Parker Palmer offers helpful elaboration, here:

"Bone-deep knowledge of resurrection would take away the fears that some of us presently use to justify our cautious, self-protecting lives. Death-dealing fear would be replaced by life giving faith...Perhaps we would be compelled to take in a homeless person; to go to prison in protest of nuclear madness; to leave jobs that contribute to violence; to speak "truth to power" in a hundred risky ways. In the process, we might lose much of what we have, perhaps even our lives—and that is the threat of resurrection...

(And within) physics nothing in the universe is ever lost, that the universe today contains the same number of atoms it had at the beginning...When a log burns in the fireplace, it does not disappear, but only changes form. Its basic particles change from seemingly solid matter to invisible waves of energy; they leave one constellation of reality only to be woven into another."[36]

This language harkens back to our previous discussion of death. Without death, there is no resurrection, "no rising again into life or into use again."[37] Without ending one thing, there is no space to birth the "new thing."

And if we did ascribe to perpetual life renewal, mightn't we be more lavish with our trust and our love? That nothing we offer is ever lost, even if we wait a very long time to see fruition of our best intentions.

I not-very-secretly enjoy the image of the man straining to keep one foot on the pier and one foot on the departing boat...and in the comedy version, he eventually falls into the water between the two.

Our lives are constantly moving and changing, and not under our complete control, no matter how much we do to mitigate that fact. Many never leave their carefully reinforced shore (playing it safe, instead) to try the adventure their yet uncharted lives hold out to them. And some, filled with potential and just as much fear, fall over and over again, being hoisted up by loved ones; resurrected, so they might try again.

After we've fallen off yet another dock, we can't know when a resurrection gesture might be offered in just the right way. And, once again, this leads us back to one of the most important and touchy subjects of all: Forgiveness. Of ourselves, of others, of Life.

Constricting theological stances have softened in many North American churches since the 1960s. The God of the Sistine Chapel ceiling has become more approachable; and the revolutionary idea that God deeply cares for us is more readily imaginable.

But childhood impressions die hard, and many were introduced to a strict, heavy-handed God-as-parental-figure, who was impossible to please. God might or might not forgive you. It can be utterly defeating to perceive the One who made us who we are isn't convinced we're turning out very well.

And space or lack of space to try and sometimes stumble, from those who spiritually or actually gave us human life in the first place, starts

71

us on our way. Their real-or-perceived influence never wanes; their voices stay in our heads for a lifetime, great therapy notwithstanding.

But new scholarship from modern theologians and church historians sheds welcome light on previous misunderstandings and faulty doctrine. For example, Brother Richard Rohr is one seeking to repair traditions which viewed God as a capricious judge.[13]

"As many others have said in different ways, we all seem to suffer from a tragic case of mistaken identity. Life is a matter of becoming fully and consciously who we already are, but a self that we largely do not know. *It is as though we are suffering from a giant case of amnesia.* As mentioned before, the protagonists in so many fairy tales are *already nobles, royal, daughters and sons of the king or even gods. But their identity is hidden from them, and the story line pivots around this discovery.*"[38](Italics mine.)

In thinking more deeply about the cruelty of being taught that we are born sinners, it seems more likely that if we actually had an unavoidable "flaw," it might be a case of Rohr's culture-wide

---

13 A construct created by St. Augustine in the 4th Century and ratified by the Council of Trent (1545-63), "Original Sin" was thought to be transferred from generation to generation during the sexual act that leads to conception. It was believed we were born with this sin from Adam, and it must be expunged in order for us to get into Heaven.

forgetting, or an innate inability to remember our belovedness. We simply cannot remember we are, essentially, all Beloved.

Disavowing the myth of "Original Sin" stands the idea of "earning God's favor" on its head, and the assumption becomes: *you are loved*, and the nearly-impossible challenge is to *remember it*. And, as if by Design, it then takes the Beloved Community to do the necessary reminding and reinforcing of our True Self.

While Brother Richard decides religion does this support work, in addition to healthy religious congregations, it has become time to broaden the traditional structures to a fully inclusive spiritual community. That this unlimited community, like the African tribe, might sing our song to remind us of True Self.

Which is why this chapter begins with resurrection (or perpetual forgiveness, if you will) and an assumption that there exists a beloved community within which we rise and trip and fall, and are hoisted up, to rise and try again.

For the sake of our society, especially tending well to all our children, there's an opportunity to live more fully into broader civic circles and exercise responsible leadership. And this intentional effort at greater inclusiveness need not lessen the benefits still found within traditionally nurturing spiritual groups.

Pema Chodron describes how we can think about such a broadening perspective and the personal motivation needed to welcome expansion:

"Taking responsibility for your own actions is another way of talking about awakening bodhichitta, because part of taking responsibility is the quality of being able to see things very clearly. Another part of taking responsibility is gentleness, which goes along with not judging, not calling things right or wrong, good or bad, but looking gently and honestly at yourself. Finally there is also the ability to keep going forward. It's been described before as letting go, but in some sense at a personal level it's that you can just keep on going; you don't get completely overwhelmed by this identity as a loser or a winner, the abuser or the abused, the good guy or the bad guy. You just see what you do as clearly and as compassionately as you can and then go on. The next moment is always fresh and open. You don't have to get frozen in an identity of any kind."[39]

In Western parlance, Pema is talking about rejecting socially ascribed labels and being in a mindset of perpetual curiosity and growth. But you notice the previous paragraph opens with the telling phrase that we are "taking responsibility...so we can see clearly." And in order to do that requires a level of comprehensive personal honesty, where we can walk with the flaws we see because the beauty of who we also are ultimately leads us to compassionate gentleness.

Something we might have missed in our Bible lessons is at whom Jesus directed His most severe criticism. To whom did He admonish to see the log in their own eye before railing against the splinter they noticed in another's eye? It wasn't the gentle ones; it was the one who judged others all day long with little energy left for self-awareness.

In Matthew's chapter 7 Jesus said, "Do not judge, or you too will be judged...Why do you look at the speck of sawdust in your brother's eye and pay no attention to the plank in your own eye? How can you say to your brother, "Let me take the speck out of your eye," when all the time there is a plank in your own eye?"[40]

I recently reexamined on what Jesus' life and words seemed to focus. It appears Jesus preached two overarching themes: Our belovedness in God's eyes, and perpetually practicing forgiveness of self and others for the sake of developing the Beloved Community.

We actively participate in creating the nurture of and for the community when we mindfully take personal account of our actions and intentions and forgive the places where we want to make improvements; embracing our whole journey. And when we think about others and find criticism sneaking in, we pray that they will experience relief in whatever plagues them, causing our irritation and theirs.

Knowing other people's issues are *their* issues, and that we can pray for their comfort and be freed from suffering, frees us, too. We can set both them and ourselves free. This is being responsible on a spiritual level that has paradoxical ramifications. When we accept and remove our own planks, the splinters we once noticed in other's eyes often disappear.

And in working with anti-bullying programs, it is clear no one is born a bully. And thanks to national efforts to educate us about the dynamics of learned aggression, the community can nurture those wounded children, of any age, back toward a deep redemption of True Self, to try again.

One could counter that there should be reasonable limits to forgiveness; How do we answer Justice? And that question is why what happened in 2006 at Nickel Mines, Pennsylvania is still so astonishing. Not the senseless execution-style slaying of innocent Amish school girls by a deeply wounded man who was angry with God. No, what about the immediate and complete forgiveness on the part of the Amish who immediately reached out to comfort the killer's family?

According to three Amish Lifestyle scholars, "letting go of grudges" is a deeply rooted value in Amish culture, which remembers martyrs who offered forgiveness, including Jesus himself. They explained that *the Amish willingness to forgo vengeance does not undo the tragedy or pardon the wrong, but rather constitutes a first step toward a future that is more hopeful.*[14]

The more we study the effects of forgiveness on those involved at any level of the event, the more we learn that to forgive is to reimagine life and hope *for us first*. It's always fascinated that loving others as ourselves *begins with us*, not the neighbor.

It is through cherishing our own lives that we might release others from the energy-draining vengeance we imagine for them. It takes a lot of work to keep someone captive while we go about everyday living, too.[15]

In well-documented discussions, the Amish unconditionally forgave and immediately extended compassion to the family of the shooter out of their cultural imperatives. "It's what we (by definition,) do." And the stunned little Amish children were being mentored as their innocent

---

14 Kraybill, Donald B., Steven M. Nolt, and David L. Weaver-Zercher (2007). *Amish Grace: How Forgiveness Transcended Tragedy.*

15 Nelson Mandela famously said that resentment is like you drinking poison in hopes it'll kill your enemy.

questions bubbled to the surface. They were simply informed that "this is who we are: Forgivers in the name of the God who forgives and restores us."

And in working through the loss and grief, which they continue to do, the powerful reality of their balanced perspective is a revelation of practical wisdom and group maturity passed from generation to generation: While our complete forgiveness brings us hope, it *does not undo the tragedy or pardon the wrong.*

This is the spiritual wisdom of most belief systems: for us to add to violence only darkens the darkness. There will be natural and/or spiritual consequences for the individual as Justice dynamics take their effect. For who among us can cast the first stone as a perfectly innocent judge?

Some observers suggested that the Amish can afford to turn the other cheek, and teach their children this approach, because they are protected by Lancaster County police forces down the street. And that may be true.

But the irrefutable fact remains that these people, who had ten girls shot and five die in their meek one-room schoolhouse, immediately and irrevocably forgave the man who brutally sprayed the room with their innocent children's blood.

And, to this day, welcome his family into theirs.

Still grieving, and still aware that Charles Carl Roberts IV is responsible for taking the lives of their children and the peaceful dreams of the community forever, the Amish insist on the fullness of living into hope over surrendering to the darkness of despair.

This is an example of the mature spiritual wisdom a community can exercise for the sake of itself and its neighbor; even toward a neighbor who exhibits hatefulness in the extreme. It is a constant challenge to our compassion and willingness to be engaged. Bridging work is never finished.

The Hutus and Tutsis are another example of our human struggle with imperfections; today trying to live next door to neighbors who wiped out entire families in the genocide. Under UN efforts through Truth and Justice Tribunals, tribal loyalties with deep-seated sense of identification, are even more difficult to breach on a personal level.

And the international examples of the last seventy years defy description. Today's arch-enemy is tomorrow's indispensible economic ally.

What must the young people make of our duplicity, as they pose the same questions about which we once wondered? If we bring the generations together, is there at last, a unique opportunity for us to bridge our national and international chasms?

Could we bring the wisdom of our more mature years together with the clear-eyed simplicity of youth to intentionally choose life-giving hope over settling for shadows?

It's still within our power to choose to heal, even as, together, we sing a broken-hearted Halleluiah. Liberated and restored compassionate elders, partnered with searching young people, can lead their beloved communities into the shimmering fullness of renewed Life.

CHAPTER EIGHT
THE THRILL OF IT ALL

"It is a sad waste of effort not to fire a carefully prepared glaze to its optimum temperature, and can make all the difference between a commonplace pot and a pot of distinction."[41]

Tile by Marilyn Allen

There's sophisticated experience and mature artistry embedded in this sweetly simple tile.

Wisdom voices have been walking us toward a possibility captured by Brother Richard Rohr:

"I now hope and believe that a kind of second simplicity is the very goal of mature adulthood and mature religion. Although we often use it in a derogatory way, I wonder if this was not our intuition when we spoke of older people as in a "second childhood?" Maybe that is what several poets meant when they said "the child is the father of the man?"[42]

A recently revisited story involving a hungry crowd of thousands, from John's Gospel, holds exciting revelations for modern North American Judeo-Christian thought. While this account is also told in Gospels by Mark and Matthew, in them, there is no mention of a young boy. Somehow, thousands of loaves and fish to feed the people appear from nowhere.

Perhaps only John grasped the teaching Jesus was holding out that day: the example of one child's enthusiastic generosity: The truly sweet and uncalculating inner child that still resides within each of us.

This was the radical realm of Heaven in action. A rebirth of the possibility of a Beloved Community.

Most of us grew up understanding that the loaves and fish kept magically multiplying. But what is more likely to have happened was this huge crowd of men, women, and children, would never have ventured to all-day event in the distant countryside, without taking along food in the deep pockets of their clothes.

And Jesus was calling to a renewed simplicity, a return to childlike innocence and way of living together in peace. Everyone would have what they needed in the Beloved Community.

The thrill of it all, the excitement of liberated opportunities in our mature years, is the awareness that in a quickly-lived youth we've often been misunderstood and misunderstood others. Now, being more awake, we are free to pay attention to being more deliberate in what we say and do and how we listen, and what it all may mean for everyone else.

We are freed to become more intentional and balanced. We can finally accept the reality of today, and willingly release yesterday's victimizing disappointments and tomorrow's constricting expectations. Our generosity grows in proportion to our gratitude.

Becoming wide awake in our mature years is thrilling. Paradoxically, better appreciation for how we relate to each other as adults, is also an opportunity to return to the gentleness of childlike innocence.

The deeper, new understanding of the story of the loaves and fish from a little boy's lunch being multiplied to feed over 5,000 people still delights, even without the magic tricks. It's more likely the miracle wasn't food magically *reproducing*, but food voluntarily *being revealed* in the pockets of others in the crowd, and shared, so that everyone had what they needed.

When anxious apostles made the loud request for anyone with food to come forward, can't you just see all the sensible folks, who'd planned a picnic for a day in the country to see Jesus magically heal some people, shrinking down in the grassy fields to avoid detection, deep pockets bulging under their robes? And how they must have shushed their children who knew they had food enough to share.

But somehow, this innocent boy, who hadn't yet learned he should worry about tomorrow's meals, popped up with his lunch held out freely and with earnest enthusiasm: "Yes, I have food; Look!"

Don't we remember, long ago, when we'd strain to raise our hands high in class to offer answers, or to offer to help when we knew we could? For many of us, it was long, long, ago, because we've since learned that giving enthusiastically and joyfully is for children who "don't know any better."

But we have also seen very grown up people leaving the safety and warmth of their own homes to help neighbors during floods or other disasters. At great inconvenience, expense, and sometimes even personal safety, many neighbors help neighbors. And now, even on a global scale.

Aren't our hearts warmed and our faith in human possibility renewed when we see such thoughtful outpourings of care?

The magnificent design of the loving family is expanded out to the fuller, mutually supportive community.

Over and over Jesus pointed out the children playing among the adults in the gathered crowds. See how they are? You must become, again, like one of these, or you simply won't see the community God has placed at your doorstep for embracing![16] You will scoff at the simplicity of caring for your neighbor in the same way you care for yourself. It will be foolishness to your grown up and mature sensibilities. Jesus said these things often and in many settings.

This is the radical freedom that is so simple we miss it, the daily choice we can practice or refuse: The message of human freedom is lying within the non-hierarchical spiritual design of the Beloved Community.

But we are committed to being sensible adults, as opposed to readily loving and playful children who trust things will work out. We are deeply

---

16 Interestingly, familiar modern Buddhist teachers like Pema Chodron and Cheri Huber cite these teachings from Jesus about becoming like children in their descriptions of truly happy, responsible people.

entrenched grown ups who have suffered physical and emotional suffering, after all, and cannot fathom that we can simultaneously exercise both sophisticated and innocent mindsets. Lacking imagination and cultivating a generalized fear, we create even more human misery out of our miserliness; believing there simply isn't enough to meet everyone's need.

But, we *can* be mature elders who can see again through the eyes of children, because we can *choose* to be people who intentionally embrace the fullness of life; both in exercising our leadership responsibility and willingness to play well with others.

In a fertile environment, this is a huge re-awakening. But time and space are needed for this level of reimagining. And there's far more to playing well with others than meets the casual eye: as it turns out, it's the very source of second-half-of-life energy. Fortunately, there's a practical and enjoyable way we can liberate and reenergizing our creative imagination process.

More and more researchers, from myriad fields, are discovering the vital importance of engaging in artistic creativity in order to experience the fullness of our humanity.

In first learning the specifics and endless intricacies of doing ceramic art, it felt chore-like. Like so many other endeavors, I wanted to do it well. After awhile, though, I began noticing how deeply sacred and intimate the experience was becoming. Unlike so many other parts of everyday life, it was not something by which I'd be evaluated; it made me unusually happy.

So far, no one can grade someone else's personal inspiration. Art as hobby, is a refreshing and unique way for us to grasp deep understandings of what acceptance and celebration of self can mean. What it might feel like "to embrace, own and expand beyond one's closely held and defended personal limitations...an attitude of, "If it exists in the world, it is mine." It is the deconstructing of one's illusions of understanding such that one is left with possibilities previously unimagined."[43]

In *Centering*, M.C. Richards, a potter, poet, and academic, connects the dots through well-articulating the sacred experience of human artistic expression. She says, "The artist, the poet, the maker, the true scientist, works from inspiration. What now comes to us as inspiration, so that we commonly refer to the "mysterious" processes of creation, may one day lie open to consciousness. The experience of art may train us in faculties for higher perception."[44]

And it often takes another voice, like the revolutionary theologian Matthew Fox, to spotlight the unique and shining contributions someone else offers. Here's a helpful portion he wrote for *Centering's* preface:

M.C. warns the artist that art can become merely a "trade" if the artist is not bent on a spiritual journey and has lost the sense of art as a "bridge between the visible and invisible worlds." Art serves. "Here the importance of centering seems emphatic." The artist is in touch with "the joyful breathing at our source." Art serves joy; art serves justice and compassion; art serves the poor, the oppressed, the victims of misbegotten power; art serves mysticism, a "return to our source"; art serves a living cosmology. Art is always bodily. There lies its affront to a Cartesian educational ideology and to a patriarchal satisfaction with cognitive knowledge alone, with truth in the head that never penetrates heart or body and therefore fails to heal the body politic. *Centering* is a bodily book, an incarnational work. Born of M. C.'s bodily work on the potter's wheel with the earthly substance that clay and body are. This book renders the impossible the unconsciousness of the body. It begs for the reunion of body, mind, and spirit.[45]

As a physical educator in the 1980s, my dissertation was a warning "no one wanted to hear"[17] about physical educators' failure to well-describe

---

17 Feedback from my dissertation advisor after reading the final draft.

and champion the need for children's move-
ment and body awareness as part of their overall
early education experience. Without articulate
advocates, I predicted there would be financial
cutbacks like there already were in art, music,
and drama programs.

And it happened, just as it had for the other
Humanity "electives."

So, when we are blessed with mindful and
articulate individuals like an M.C. Richards and
Matthew Fox, there's another opportunity to
rethink our choices and priorities based on a fuller
appreciation of the whole truth about implications for still-developing human beings.

Richards warns that we have "lost the sense
of art as a bridge between the visible and invisible worlds." That we are a divided people whose
very own beings are begging for "the reunion of
body, mind, and spirit."

This sounds like a vital truth that could inspire
action-taking.

There are compulsory subjects; you know them:
the ones tested on college placement exams.
And there are the "extra-curricular," expressive, and creative subjects, those considered as
nice-to-have but not the "essential" predictors of
social success.

And each and every distinctly different society decides for its children what defines "success" for them, doesn't it? Human limitations are culturally restricted from our earliest beginnings. And in a globally interconnected world, arbitrary limits make less and less sense; and our children see this and wonder.

So, there's a renewed opportunity to repeat that we human beings ignore our mind or body or spirit, and their life-affirming intersections, at our peril.[18] There's another chance to experience deep reflection and truth making through personal exploration by means of creative expression.

It is an important part of the journey to explore both loss and gratitude to discover we are not alone. Don't we wish we'd earlier realized it is a courageous and necessary thing to respect and relinquish our disappointments in order to go deeper into what's real and discover deep peace; to see how very interconnected we all are? To know the radically whole truth sets us free.

It is a paradox we cannot well explain but seems absolutely true. Perhaps M.C. Richards' words can further expand the dynamic:

---

18 And as vulgar as separating ourselves into three compartments of mind-body-spirit sounds, it is the currently acceptable construct we understand and with which we can work.

I am brought to a crisis of conscience...when separation and, more seriously, estrangement occur, whether in a relationship of personal regard or public encounter. I am brought to a crisis because I am committed to acceptance and to the suffering it entails. I have to accept the separation in order to keep contact with the shape the experience is taking: I must keep my clay centered. The natural changes can take place only if I do not stand in the way of the flow of energy. In order to accept mistrust, I have to experience *that* and live into *its* meaning. Acceptance is not a nod of civility, nor is it approval. It is something more like ingestion, a capacity to experience the reality of another not as if it were one's own but indeed as another's, a capacity for self-surrender to the reality of another person (this is surrender not of the will, but of the perception)...The flame of our meeting burns...and it is a difficult fire to bear, and I feel the strain. It is the strain of keeping together rather than keeping apart.

In this centering which potters perform with clay, poet with music and imagery, person with conscience and consciousness....Transformations in pottery, poetry, and the person come about in experiences which centers the dualisms, the flying parts, the stragglers.

In these moments of crisis, we are at sea, unwell, discouraged but somehow resolute....

We do not stroll gaily and confidently down life's path, merrily sowing seeds of wisdom and contentment and merrily reaping their harvest. This ecology we are involved in operates by no such simple design. The facts of life are hard.

It helps, I think, to consider ourselves on a very long journey: the main thing is to keep to the path, to endure, to help each other when we stumble or tire, to weep and press on. Perhaps if I had a coat of arms, this would be my motto: Weep and begin again.

I have to yield myself to the transforming condition of love. It is a frightening and sacred moment. There is no return. It is the fire that gives us our shape.[46]

The thrill of it all; the breathtaking rollercoaster ride of exhilaration and terror and exhilaration again is the adventure that is our human experience.

And note again Richards' mature wisdom, echoing the Amish culture, in saying, "Acceptance (of difficult disappointments in our lives) is not a nod of civility, nor is it approval... the main thing is to keep to the path, to endure, to help each other when we stumble or tire, to weep and press on."

We are not designed to live in isolation; to be rigidly independent and silent children, frenetic adults, and silenced elders awaiting death. We are born creative, expressive, and full of capacity for community for a lifetime.

Of his own journey, gifted psychologist John Bradshaw said,

"There I was in a Roman Catholic seminary where everyone was doing work on St. Thomas Aquinas and I was studying the writings of Nietzsche, the philosopher who pronounced the "death of God." I remember how moved I was when I first read these lines from one of Nietzsche's letters:

If these Christians want me to believe in their god, they'll have to sing me better songs; they'll have to look more like people who have been saved; they'll have to wear on their countenance the joy of the beatitudes. I could only believe in a god who dances.

A god who dances! A god who is joyous and celebrates life! The old order crucifies all of us for expressing our I AMness and creativity."[47]

Music! Joy! Dance! For Nietzsche, these would reflect the thrill of the fullness of life of a regenerated child of wonder in a mature adult. This inner child would motivate each of us to co-create with the One who is the source of our very breath. We would express Life's Mystery in unlimited ways.

It seems the point of the exercise, for those with eyes to see and ears to hear, is to share all of Life's mysterious richness within the Beloved Community our whole lives long. In deepest humility and with compassion refined in the fire of our own hard-won peace, we joyfully help each other make meaning and connections, every step of the way.

The matured community members, who hold the sacred wisdom and redemption found in appreciating their own lives, can deliberately offer balanced eldership and hope-filled comfort as a light on the path to the young people, who are just beginning the mysterious and holy exploration that is life abundant.

CHAPTER NINE
THE POINT OF THE EXERCISE

"Unlike the medical student, who learns about the body before getting on to the general practice of curing maladies and weaknesses, most potters learn about their materials by trying to cure faults."[48]

Potter and mentor, Peggy Loudon's hands guide another's budding exploration.

Just as master potters become teacher-guides for beginning artists, an apparent goal of our lives is to become fully awake for ourselves and others. Since we share a human limitation of not being able to see very far down the path before we're committed to the journey, it's good to know, in the second half of life, that we are freer to see with wide-opened eyes and so better able to appreciate and describe the unfolding masterpiece that is our life.

It is from this broader perspective that we might gently mentor others. And exercising mature and joyful responsibility for wise community eldership may well be the point of the second half of our lives.

Brother Richard Rohr offers this vital observation about a mentor's perspective:

"Ironically, we are more than ever before in a position to change people---but we do not need to---and that makes all the difference. We have moved from doing to being to an utterly new kind of doing that flows almost organically, quietly, and by osmosis. Our actions are less compulsive. We do what we are called to do, and then try to let go of the consequences. We usually cannot do that very well when we are young."[49]

It takes extraordinary self-awareness, especially the exercise of choosing how we go about remembering our lives, to become effective mentors to others. If we are diligent in our remembering, working well with our "unfinished business," we will come away with a greater perspective on our shared humanity and need for personal humility. Compassionate humility is essential. Embracing the thrill of is all is our birthright.

Relinquishing the resentment of our disappointed hopes, dreams, and expectations in favor of accepting how life has actually played out, makes way for the mature hopefulness younger people crave to see. Only when we do this deep relinquishment can we offer eyes-wide-open truth to others. This deliberate and sacred process of beholding our memories is often painful, because it is the purifying fire that transforms and enlivens.

One of the priceless surprises of doing deep life review work is we see multitudes of blessings and are overwhelmed by personal gratitudes. We learn from where our hope comes; we can describe how resilience was developed and share these greatest of gifts.

So, there must be a deliberately chosen shift from apprentice to craftsman for us to do what our second half of life offers; a willingness to come to terms with and embrace Life's necessary suffering to discover deep peace.

This book was created to deliberately walk us toward a healthy capacity to remember our lives well, that is, with a fully accepting, spiritually balanced, and intentionally gentle perspective. This process gives us the authentic integrity needed to develop trust between a mentor and protégée.

Fully remembering and processing our life's myriad events, so another might be encouraged into an exciting future of possibilities based on the mentor's hard-won wisdom, is priceless.

Elders often remark they are intimidated by the thought of mentoring another person. By not knowing what mentoring might entail, out of innocent ignorance, they then wonder if "they even have anything relevant to offer." These next few pages are devoted to a very brief introduction to mentoring, which may serve to help put those unnecessary assumptions aside.

The popular definition of mentor is simply, "A trusted counselor or guide. It is a relationship in which a person with greater experience and wisdom guides another person to develop both personally and professionally. Mentoring helps prepare people for the increased responsibilities they will assume as they progress."

Our young people are justifiably confused when they shoulder responsibilities far beyond the wisdom and experience of their years. The challenges they face are mammoth in scale: pollution of air, land, and waters; global connectivity that displays through daily media, the vividly gross injustices and inequities around their world; and our vulnerabilities to natural disasters and reexamination of traditional spiritual beliefs, to name only a few of the destabilizing and morally eroding fundamentals with which they are expected to walk without despairing.

How can they possibly hold all this? With the matured community elder's supportive companionship.

One of the deepest desires of grounded young people is to become wise. So, how might mentors offer another person the development of wisdom? In addition to sharing our own helpful experiences, which is the foundation of a mentoring relationship, is there a teachable, time-tested approach to the way we tell our stories, (e.g. process our lives,) which might help young people become both resilient and wise?

In the practice of discernment, there is an emerging decision-making discipline that's every bit as practical as it is spiritually grounding. Doctor Elizabeth Liebert is a trusted discernment advocate and teacher. Currently serving as Dean of a dynamic Northern California seminary, she masterfully moves between the practical and spiritual realms in her own demanding life; making her counsel especially note worthy by mentors of all persuasions:

"We are creatures whose deepest self-realization comes from moving into God's future with all the life and skill with which we have been endowed, within the concrete situations of our particular and finite lives. Our fulfillment, then, lies in becoming the deepest, most alive person that we can be and that our concrete situations will allow."[50]

While there are many approaches to discernment, the seven steps Dr. Liebert advocates, particular spiritual language notwithstanding, resonate with students of problem-solving and decision-making in any field. Additionally, the spiritual aspect can bring another layer of benefit to the mentor and their student: the development of wisdom.

1) Seek spiritual freedom, the inner disposition upon which discernment rests and which creates the climate for discernment[19]; 2) Discover and name the issue you face (what's really going on is not always obvious); 3) Gather and evaluate appropriate data about the issue; 4) Reflect and pray (slow down and reconnect to deeper spirituality); 5) Formulate a tentative decision (there are many methods by which we can come to decisions); 6) Seek confirmation (what do other trusted people think of your idea and do you sense a spiritual confirmation yourself?); 7) Assess the process (Was there a point without freedom, peace, or calm?)

Ultimately, time reveals the fruit of discernment. And Dr. Liebert concludes, "This final look back

---

19 Liebert notes this is where the seeker deliberately seeks the greater good beyond only their personal benefit

can deepen our conviction that we have chosen with deep integrity...Nothing need be lost."[51]

There are many benefits to leaning into such a life choices process as a discipline, rather than the often last resort "pro-con" list[20]. A young person working through this deliberation approach with a trusted mentor's support is ideal. And the young person experiences their whole being, mind, body, and spirit, playing its part in making life-forming choices.

From uncertain beginnings, young people learn to trust themselves because "nothing need be lost." In the Beloved Community, nothing in life is wasted. Every choosing event becomes part of personal growth and community history. It is living out the fullness of our humanity together.

And through mentoring others in the discernment process, elders remember the purpose of their own journey through these pages of metaphor and ceramic process: we can appreciate and celebrate anew the miraculous unfolding of the uniquely journeyed paths of our good (enough) lives.

---

20 In creating a "pro-con list" when faced with a difficult decision, the person makes a line down the middle of a sheet of paper; one column labeled "pro" for positives about going ahead, and "con" for reasons to the contrary. After looking at the quality and quantity of each side, the person makes their decision.

As elders invest time in upcoming community leaders, they have the freedom to rejoice in the redemption of their own earlier, murkier days of uncertainty; the journey through those many intimidating trees in the forest along their previously uncharted road less travelled.

And these thoughtful mentors become those who cast a bright light further down the young person's life path than the young person could possibly cast by themselves.

Interestingly, major corporations are actively partnering with high schools to improve student's basics like: English, math, science and technology. But they also note a great need for the interpersonal, professional skills that ensure young people's ability to make their way in the most challenging environments.

They realize these youngsters benefit from the human stories out of elders' experiences.

New leaders need specific "people skills" to thrive in the global community and within large structures like Inter-Governmental Organizations, non-profits, and other businesses. They'll need the basics of team work: leading and following; how to present an idea to an already overly-taxed supervisor; how to share credit; and what to do when values clash between workers, and workers and supervisors. And so forth.

Pockets of community elders are being formally asked to volunteer to mentor in one or both arenas: "practical" skills along with the interpersonal. Corporate America recognizes that the young people need the confidence-building their relationship to an authentic and compassionate person who's "been there" might provide.

Some of the most poignant character qualities are best taught by someone completely outside "the formal corporate system," who will not financially benefit from the care they extend. They mentor as a privilege of life in the community, as our Native Americans and many other indigenous peoples demonstrate, in passing on tribal stories and personal experience.

We are better mentors when, fully and gently, we remember our own earlier frustrations and tears long since replaced by eventual satisfactions and joys that came with a matured perspective. It's important to remember that we learned more when freed to form our own questions and come to personal "working definitions."

Like many, I rashly believed I'd done much of my life on my own and on my own terms. As a young person, I was spinning too fast to appreciate the quiet and gently supportive hands all around me. In finally slowing down and better remembering those frenetic days, I was clearly surrounded by like-minded souls. Many mentors worked even harder, sacrificing even more, than I.

Such is the foolish, but seemingly necessary, narcissism of youth. And it is the privilege of maturity to gain a balance view, and a healthy community dynamic to offer this wiser perspective as possibility and hope to the next generation.

And, not surprisingly, in order for mentors to land in this space of peace and resolve is, once again, an observation about deep acceptance and forgiveness. Elders who bring their unfinished angers and resentments into mentoring can do great harm to a tender, trust-based relationship.

A popular new definition of deep forgiveness is lovingly "letting go of any possibility of having had a different (or better) past."[21] It is the work of accepting the real and letting go of our disappointments.

As you see, we're again noting resentment dynamics. But this time, we distinctly wrestle with it for the sake of the younger generation. Before we can well mentor another, we must face the still-unfinished tales in our own history; forgive ourselves and others in how things actually played-out, and then, one-by-one, let all the disappointments and attachments go. Let it all be what

---

21 Cited sources are mixed, including Lily Tomlin, Anne Lamott, Rabbi Kushner, and Oprah Winfrey.

really happened, as best we can hold it. And let all of the perfect imperfection of our lives benefit others in the community, as their magnificence also benefits us.

This boss, that teacher, that pastor, our mom, dad, grandparents...no one lived up to their role definitions perfectly. Because we are all human, the lament that "Eventually, everybody lets you down," appears true. Once again, our expectations are a perfect set-up for disappointment.

But, without lofty goals and hopes and dreams, would we be fully human?

And so we wrestle with this paradox as we travel our path and negotiate both the joys of great relationships and achievements, as well as unraveling and grieving the occasional surprises that send us reeling. It is all part of how life requires our humility and perpetual forgiveness of self and others on the journey toward becoming authentically compassionate.

So if someone comes to you for advice, upon what is your counsel based? Have you yet come to terms with the "good enoughness" of your bosses, teachers, family members, and friends, Pastor or Rabbi or Imam? Have you forgiven their human frailty and your own? Have you lovingly let go of any possibility of having had a different past?

The opportunity in second-half-of-life remembering is to gain peaceful wisdom and a future of hope through intentionally holding where and how we've been. Deliberately gentle remembering is what we can cull and then share with searching youth.

Out of our authentic lives we can speak a deep truth that is refreshing and life-giving. If we do the work it takes to free our True Self, we live in our community long after we've moved on. Our lives become a permanent facet of the larger culture that defines our particular community.

Culture experts like Edgar Schein (1985) describe how a society is most easily recognized by the easily observable, but not explicitly defined, "artifacts" like people's interpersonal behavior and things people use every day.

Outsiders *infer* values and beliefs from conversations with people from a different culture. But, according to Schein, being absolutely *certain* what drives another culture's values and beliefs is not possible, because of the Underlying Assumptions. And even within the culture, these assumptions are ill-defined.

Mentors help make explicit what seems inferred or implied about what our culture values, and is often confusing to young leaders. Becoming an elder, and so, a mentor to the next generation, depends on both preparation and willingness to embrace the honor of the responsibility of mentoring future leaders.

There is sacred trust in the journey, with each part of a person's life having vital meaning and great consequence for the health and overall well-being of the tribe. With a thoughtful mentor's help, a protégée can formulate questions that most need addressing and draft a gently balanced and an ink-never-dried notional blueprint for their own life's journey.

Young people, encouraged by mature mentors to learn how to discern among life's options, will likely recognize better life choices as, more and more, they wake up to their own lives.

And we are certainly experiencing a wake-up-call time. We are noticing the sheer pace at which we live is pulling us farther and farther from those we need and love most. And, importantly, our perception of what success and personal wealth mean is coming under scrutiny. We have a rare opportunity to think about our lives and what we want them to mean for those who are waiting for us to grow into eldership. We can still shape the world we want to leave for others.

As discussed, it takes extraordinary self-awareness in how we go about remembering our lives to become peace-filled elders and truly effective mentors. The more intentionally balanced our remembering, the greater is our sense of shared humanity, compassion, and abundant gratitude.

The most effective mentoring comes from a gentle humility: a balanced personal perspective and awareness of our interconnectedness to everything. If we are willing to be gentle, but completely honest with the "ups and downs" of our lives, then we have a comprehensive truth to offer others. Both our past "brilliant successes" and "abysmal failures" are of equal importance to someone still trying to establish their sense of direction. And seeing you are "still standing" is hopefulness personified.

It is out of the radical truth of our whole lives that we become a role model, teacher and coach. It is out of a personal commitment to another person that we might become their mentor.

Establishing authentic and caring relationships is the heart of forming pockets of resilience in a community. This is the essence of effective mentoring between leaders and developing leaders: Between elders and young people. And, it is a responsibility of the older generation to the younger.

In a new book called *Everyone Leads*, Public Allies leader Paul Schmitz offers poignant researched observations about the facts of leadership, and our modern young people:

"We talk about leadership in terms of an action one takes, not in terms of a position one holds. Leadership is about taking responsibility---both personal and social---for working with others on shared goals. Everyone has some circle of influence where it is possible to take responsibility for leading.

In the so-called Millenials, we have a new generation whose members have a strong interest in community service (research shows they have volunteered more than previous generations), embrace diversity (this is the most diverse generation to date), and prefers to work in teams.

Technology does not have to replace face-to-face interaction as some fear or criticize, but often accelerates or enhances it...social networking sites...allow us to rebuild, albeit virtually, the kind of old rural communities where everyone knew everyone else.

In terms of organizing for change---technology is a crucial tool for leadership and mobilization."[52]

Our Millenial youngsters are just like we were at their age, but their idea of their community is vaster than ours was, and the pace at which they take in unfiltered information is mindboggling. But they are still young people who need help putting all this stimulation into useful "buckets" for processing, retention, and most importantly, elimination.

For all their super-sonic, sophisticated technology, our young people especially now, need community elders to walk with them as mentors.

It's the natural role for those with more experience to guide those with less. The nature of modern-day problems; their complexity and rate of lightning-fast change creates an entirely new dynamic where there is greater give-and-take between an elder and their protégée. And because human beings are so multi-faceted, it's reasonable to expect the presence of multiple mentors in one young person's life.

Our youth deserve opportunities for mature elder mentoring. Elders deserve opportunities to be heard as they find their mentoring "voice." The effectiveness of each mentoring relationship is played out over time, with give-and-take on everyone's part, and may take adjustments to find good matches.

Elders certainly aren't expected to have everything resolved in order to answer this call to community leadership; our lives continue to be works-in-progress! But there are deeply personal questions for potential mentors to first discern.

Do we want to model, as imperfectly as we did and still do, what it might mean to pursue a balanced life, through cultivating a wide-open perspective on the fullness of life, including our own rich spirituality and personal involvement in creative expression and physical well-being? Are we committed to the future of the community where we live and feel drawn, to then imbue the young people with self-respect and respect for all living things?

Pragmatically, are you an elder who might try to show someone how trust-building comes from personal integrity and a lean-forward commitment to developing mindful relationships with co-workers and supervisors; working intentionally every day, and asking for necessary training to anticipate future needs? Would you teach a young person that developing his or her ability to be an independent critical thinker on behalf of the too-busy leader is one of the greatest assets workers can offer?[22]

And, would you try to patiently guide a young person toward formulation of their own good questions as they seek deeper understandings and direction?[23]

---

22 See Colin Powell's opinions on the critical value of dissent, and Robert E. Kelley's Dimensions of Followership.

23 This approach to mentoring is at the heart of Spiritual Direction, where a trained and often supervised mentor listens to the mentee as they seek to discern the deeper questions along life's journey. People of all ages receive great benefits as mentees from this respectful relationship. A global and robustly diverse organization called *Spiritual Directors International* can be reached for further information at www.sdiworld.org.

Innovative ideas are coming from the young-est and least formally experienced people. Some will never "earn their stripes" in the tradition way; they won't neatly climb the rungs of the tradition-ally-prescribed corporate ladder. Instead, they'll find themselves leading others soon after formal education ends. The new organization charts often aren't vertical or linear.

These particularly bright young people are especially in need of a safe place to land; *a person* who can steady them as from day one, they are sprinting. As sophisticated and "together" as they might seem, young people have only the years of life they have lived and no more. They cannot yet do this alone.

Their technological (gadgets galore) and global awareness (Facebook friends in faraway places, Wikipedia data at the touch of a button) savvy can intimidate tribal elders. But they are still young; they cannot sustain their current pace without a serious crash. And self-aware elders know that.

The young people have grown up with tech-nology and instant connection and getting far too much instant global news, unfiltered for age-appropriate absorption. This is their "normal."

But, they are our children, meaning, they are not yet far evolved from where their community elders are sitting and experiencing life as human beings. The pace is too much for their minds and hearts and bodies, too. They will stress out, burn out, and despair, as have many of their Baby Boomer parents.

Our young people are growing up without global and workplace precedence. Referring to vastly diverse issues, we constantly hear, "We've never seen anything like this before."

From climate change to disease and natural disaster management to Arab Spring to China's economic position in the world to global political interconnectivity and immediate access to anyone at anytime, elders-in-charge are not well deciphering or anticipating lightning-fast world changes, so it's unconscionably left to the young people to get themselves prepared based on the best available economic projections.

The mentoring connection, by thinking beyond only the financial implications in global dynamics, can bridge the generations and yield a wise way forward to benefit everyone.

And the mentoring relationship simply boils down to a searching younger person spending time with an authentically mature and respectful tribal elder for mutual storytelling, creative imagining, and a gaining of wisdom through the discernment discipline. Needs beyond the scope of the relationship are met by others, as well as seeking needed formal training or education.

As elders reexamine and explore their lives through healing conversations and relationships and creative expression, they can embody and demonstrate the joy of being human. They can, at last, live out a balance and sweetness that eluded them in their younger, more frenetic days.

What we believe about our value to others depends simply on a willingness to remain dynamically connected to the Beloved Community, beyond our family of origin. And this offers hopeful encouragement to our young people, as intention is nearly everything in their intergenerational relationships.

And finally, when tribal elders who have mentored out of the fullness of their good (enough) lives, circle back around to the physical helplessness of the newborn, the community is privileged to witness the truest and most natural course of human events. Our perfect imperfection invites us to marvel and learn and continue to care for each other, as we live through all of our very human life with grateful eyes, wide open.

And we discover that we are good (enough) people who need not be afraid. We have found, and have helped sustain, our earthly home.

ENDNOTES

Introduction

1 Muller, Kristin, The Potter's Studio Handbook (Beverly, Massachusetts: Quarry Books, 2007), 54.

Chapter One

2 Ibid, 9.

3 Beck, Martha, Finding Your Way in a Wild New World: Reclaim Your True Nature to Create the Life You Want (New York: Simon and Schuster, 2012), Kindle location 3744.

4 Palmer, Parker J., Let Your Life Speak (San Francisco: Jossey-Bass, 2000), 66-67.

5 Birks, Tony, The Complete Potter's Companion (New York: Bulfinch Press, 2003), 9.

Chapter Two

6 Muller, Kristin, The Potter's Studio Handbook (Beverly, Massachusetts: Quarry Books, 2007), 16.

7 Rohr, Richard, Falling Upward: Spirituality for the Two Halves of Life (San Francisco: Jossey-Bass, 2011), 94.

8 Ibid, 88-89.

Chapter Three

9 Birks, Tony, The Complete Potter's Companion (New York: Bulfinch Press, 2003), 16.

10 Rohr, Richard, Falling Upward: Spirituality for the Two Halves of Life (San Francisco: Jossey-Bass, 2011), 86.

11 Ibid, 85.

12 Palmer, Parker, A Hidden Wholeness: The Journey Toward an Undivided Life (San Francisco: Jossey-Bass, 2004), 90.

13 Ibid, 91.

14 Merton, Thomas, New Seeds of Contemplation (New York: New Directions Books, 1962), 38.

15 Chodron, Pema, The Wisdom of No Escape (Boston: Shambhala Publications, Inc., 2001), 69.

16 Ibid, 96.

Chapter Four

17 Birks, Tony, The Complete Potter's Companion (New York: Bulfinch Press, 2003), 21.

18 Webster's College Dictionary (New York: Federal Street Press, 2003), 204.

19 Ibid, 323.

20 Chodron, Pema, The Places That Scare You (Boston: Shambhala Publications, Inc., 2001), 119.

21 Ibid, 120.

22 Ibid, 121-2.

23 Ibid, 21-22.

24 Rohr, Richard, Falling Upward: Spirituality for the Two Halves of Life (San Francisco: Jossey-Bass, 2011), 73-4.

Chapter Five

25 Muller, Kristin, The Potter's Studio Handbook (Beverly, Massachusetts: Quarry Books, 2007), 45-6.

26 Chodron, Pema, The Wisdom of No Escape (Boston: Shambhala Publications, Inc., 2001), 14.

27 Ibid, 15.

28 Mellody, Pia, Facing Codependence (New York: Harper Collins Publishers, 2003), 50-1.

Chapter Six

29 Birks, Tony, The Complete Potter's Companion (New York: Bulfinch Press, 2003), 181.

30 Bourgeault, Cynthia, Mystical Hope (Lanham, Maryland: Rowman and Littlefield, 2001), 68-9.

31 Harrison, Steven, Doing Nothing (Boulder, CO: Sentient Pub., 2008), 118-119.

32 Tolle, Eckhart, A New Earth (New York: Plume Books, 2005), 127-8.

33 Palmer, Parker, The Active Life (San Francisco: Jossey-Bass, 1990), 155-7.

34 Rohr, Richard, Falling Upward: Spirituality for the Two Halves of Life (San Francisco: Jossey-Bass, 2011), 50-1.

Chapter Seven

35 Muller, Kristin, The Potter's Studio Handbook (Beverly, Massachusetts: Quarry Books, 2007), 56-7.

36 Palmer, Parker, The Active Life (San Francisco: Jossey-Bass, 1990), 153; 149-50.

37 Webster's College Dictionary (New York: Federal Street Press, 2003), 767.

38 Rohr, Richard, Falling Upward: Spirituality for the Two Halves of Life (San Francisco: Jossey-Bass, 2011), 97.

39 Chodron, Pema, Start Where You Are (Boston: Shambhala Publications, Inc., 2001), 109.

40 The Harper Collins Study Bible, NRSV (New York, NY: Harper Collins Publishers, 1993), 1869-70.

Chapter Eight

41 Birks, Tony, The Complete Potter's Companion (New York: Bulfinch Press, 2003), 139.

42 Rohr, Richard, Falling Upward: Spirituality for the Two Halves of Life (San Francisco: Jossey-Bass, 2011), 109.

43 Huber, Cheri, When You're Falling, Dive: Acceptance, Freedom and Possibility (Keep It Simple Books, 2003), 2-3.

44 Richards, M.C., Centering: In Pottery, Poetry, and the Person (Middletown, CT: Wesleyan University Press, 1989), 94.

45 Ibid, xv.

46 Ibid, 140-141.

47 Bradshaw, John, Homecoming: Reclaiming and Championing Your Inner Child (New York: Bantam Books, 1990), 274.

Chapter Nine

48 Birks, Tony, The Complete Potter's Companion (New York: Bulfinch Press, 2003), 137.

49 Rohr, Richard, Falling Upward: Spirituality for the Two Halves of Life (San Francisco: Jossey-Bass, 2011), 123.

50 Liebert, Elizabeth, The Way of Discernment: Spiritual Practices for Decision-Making (Louisville: Westminister John Knox Press, 2008), 18.

51 Ibid, 21.

52 Schmitz, Paul, Everyone Leads (San Francisco: Jossey-Bass, 2012), xv, 9, 70.

Artists credited in this book may be reached through the Arcata Fire Arts Center in Arcata, California at (707) 826-1445; 520 South G Street, Arcata, CA 95521; or fireartsarcata.com.